FUTURE OF THE FAMILY

edited by

FUTURE
OF THE FAMILY

edited by
Clayton C. Barbeau

The Bruce Publishing Company/New York
Collier-Macmillan Limited/London

301.42
F996

The Publisher and the Editor wish to thank
WAY—Catholic Viewpoints in whose pages some of
the material in this book was first published.

72-338

THE BRUCE PUBLISHING COMPANY, NEW YORK
COLLIER-MACMILLAN CANADA, LTD., TORONTO, ONTARIO

Made in the United States of America

CONTENTS

INTRODUCTION: WHATEVER HAPPENED TO JANE EYRE?

Clayton C. Barbeau

One hundred and twenty years ago *Jane Eyre,* a novel then considered impious by some, was published. Keystone of the plot was the dilemma confronting Jane and Rochester. Deeply in love with one another, they are unable to marry because Rochester already is married to a lunatic, an impediment Jane discovers only during the course of the ceremony in which Rochester is about to (bigamously) marry her. After this event, as all readers of the novel will recall, he asks Jane to leave the country with him, to become his mistress. Rochester tells how he was deluded into marrying the already unbalanced woman, describing it as a marriage in name only. He proclaims his true love for Jane; she does not doubt his word. He offers undying faithfulness to her; she believes he means it. She knows that he is the only person in the world who cares for her. Rochester pleads, even threatens suicide, should she turn him down, but Jane refuses to become his mistress. She refuses, as she put it, to break a law made by God, sanctioned by men. Since Rochester is married, Jane sees only one course open to her: she departs.

When a group of eighth graders in a Catholic school were discussing this novel, the first question they asked was: "Why didn't he get a divorce?" What was unthinkable for Charlotte Brontë, the authoress; for Jane Eyre, her orphaned heroine; for Rochester, her wealthy hero; and for all the readers of *Jane Eyre* for some years after the book's publication, was the first thought of a group of today's children.

In a little over a century, we have moved from a period during which divorce was not only considered against God's law but was not on the statute books in many lands, to a time during which divorce is present at every wedding ceremony. Divorce may be openly present, as in a recent marriage when the partners agreed beforehand to a divorce in a year "if it doesn't work out"; it may be a hidden reservation, a back door one or the other has left open in case the worse exceeds the better in the marriage. More often it is simply part of the social context in which the vow "till death do us part" is taken—an invisible, not consciously recognized, but nonetheless present and influential part of the ecology of family life today. For any and every marriage contracted today divorce, as a possibility, is part of the landscape.

Something else has changed in the last century, too. Romantic love of the sort Rochester and Jane experienced was not, even in that day, considered a necessary ingredient to a successful marriage. As Joan Bel Geddes and the Birds, among others, point out, romantic love has been in ages past considered something of a luxury. It was quite thinkable for persons not romantically inclined toward each other to marry and to have a stable and even happy home life. Indeed, a recent newspaper story of a young immigrant to America going home to marry the bride his family had chosen for him and being quite pleased with their choice, accentuates the fact that in many parts of the world marriages are still arranged on grounds other than romantic love.

Romantic love has been with man since earliest times (consider the love story of Jacob and Rachel in the Old Testament), but it seldom has been, in the past, considered essential to matrimony. Few of the love sonnets of even the Christian poets of the Middle Ages were written to their wives. In Dante's day, the courtly love code explicitly denied the possibility of a man being able to love his wife for the simple reason that she *was* his wife. St. Thomas More's second marriage was contracted within a year after his first wife died, because he needed a wife to manage his household and a woman's hand with his children. Yet, in our own day, it would be considered unthinkable—or at least cold-blooded—for either party to enter a marriage admitting that he was not "in love" with the other person.

At the same time, the mass media, both in entertainment features and advertising, feed the flames of romantic desire, nourish the daydreams of romantic hopes, and constantly hold out the promise of a lifetime of romantic love through the making of the "right" marriage match. Notwithstanding the unrealism of most of this trivia, millions are influenced by it. The emotional demands that many place upon their marriages as a result are crushing; crushing enough to fill the offices of marriage counselors and divorce lawyers for reasons undreamt of when this century began.

Rev. Paul Marx and Jack Quesnell describe a series of social revolutions, all of which affect the family. One of these is the Erotic Revolution. Seventy years ago books were published that stated as a matter of fact that no woman, save a harlot, would look for sexual pleasure. However ignorant we consider the authors, they were stating a commonly held belief which few of their contemporaries or predecessors would challenge.

The men of only a generation ago who were working thirteen hours a day, six-and-a-half days a week, and their wives who were caught up in the seven day a week survival and maintenance chores at home, had little time to reflect upon the quality of their sexual intercourse, to consciously question whether or not they were sexually fulfilled. Today, for many, sexual pleasure is one of the major tests of their marital success. Indeed, so much does sexual satisfaction dominate the contemporary notion of marriage that we have shelves of books called "marriage manuals" which are not about marriage or family life at all, but about human anatomy and, particularly, genital organs and various postures for their pleasurable use.

The acceptance of divorce, the identification of romantic love with marital happiness, and the demand for sexual satisfaction are only three of the more obvious influences which make contemporary marriages different from those of the past. Another influence, touched upon by Janet Golden and Sidney Callahan, is the new-found independence of women and, indeed, the adjustment of the marital relationship to this reality. As the Birds point out, there was an economic basis for most marriages in the past. Job opportunities for women were scarce. The unmarried woman either was the maiden aunt (built-in baby-sitter for her married kin), a nun, a governess (like Jane Eyre), or she starved. Marriage meant she had a provider and in return she provided the various necessary household services and, for that matter, children. Obviously, this is no longer true.

Jobs for women exist, educational opportunities abound, and even the woman who desires to work at home finds herself with time to devote to the larger community and to develop her personal talents. Marriages where the wife makes more money than her husband are not uncommon. Recently I met a woman novelist who deliberately had kept her second book unpublished because her husband's first had yet to find a publisher. This situation is dramatically different from the day when Charlotte Brontë had to publish under the man's name of Currer Bell because women could not be writers.

The shift in roles, given immense impetus during and just after World War II, has not come easily for some. There are men who resist it instinctively because of their rigid notions of what the marital roles should be, concepts gleaned from their parents' (i.e., residual Victorian) marriage, or because they feel threatened by the prospect of a wife not being dependent upon them economically, or for other such reasons. The tension and difficulties that can be caused by the clash between a husband's desire to have his wife fulfill a certain wifely role and his wife's desire to be herself, are relatively new problems besetting marriage.

We have so far touched upon only a few of the factors that presently are influencing the marital relationship itself, and have not yet mentioned the family unit. Marriage becomes familial when the relationship of the two opens itself to include others. One of the basic familial relationships is that of parent and child. There is no more challenging work in the world today, nor a work more demanding of intelligence, tact, humor, perspective, wholeness, compassion, true faith, and lively hope than that of parenthood. Never in history has a generation of parents had to cope with a generation of children who have had so many sources of information, education and entertainment independent of, beyond the control of, and sometimes at variance with their parents.

Though the tension between fathers and sons has been one of the constants of Western literature, from *Antigone* through the *New Testament,* from *Romeo and Juliet* through *Fathers and Sons* to Herb Gold's *The Fathers,* the bald truth is that contemporary parents confront children born and raised in an entirely different world than that in which their own attitudes were formed.

The average parent of, say, forty-five, was born of parents and educated in his earliest years by teachers who were themselves mature in their ideas before the time of the electric light, the automobile, the radio, the airplane, and World War I. This means that many of the basic ideals of today's parents are the fruit of assumptions and attitudes planted in early youth and are recognizably Victorian in regard to sex, nationalistic in regard to patriotism, punitive in regard to misdeeds, and puritan in regard to work and play. They may have been raised in a home where "children are to be seen and not heard," and where masculine and feminine roles were sharply defined. They may have struggled in their youthful days to help support the family in the time of the Depression and thereby learned to link education with job qualifications (one major oil company in those days would only hire B.A.s to man its pumps). They viewed service in World War II or Korea as a duty to country, a dirty job that had to be done and one which few, if any, would question. Especially in regard to the Second World War, they had no misgivings: the bombing of Pearl Harbor, the horrors being perpetrated by Hitler on innocent people demanded that honorable men take action. They came home to the GI Bill, which gave them the education that before would have been out of their reach. They went through school with the help of their wives (who earned the PHT—Putting Hubby Through—diploma) and into the profession for which they had trained themselves. Then they worked like hell to make up for lost time. They also had their first children while in school, again to make up for the lost time.

The children born since World War II—over one third of this nation's present population was born after the death of Hitler—entered a world where television was available as soon as they were able to look at it. They entered a world where the atom bomb (which Daddy hailed as a swift end to a long and bloody conflict) spelled the possible end of the planet. They grew up in a more permissive school system, a more relaxed home atmosphere, and a more affluent society than their parents. Indeed, the magazine route Daddy had during the depression no longer existed as a job; most jobs for youths were gone. Where Daddy had saved his money to buy a jalopy that didn't work and had to labor to make it run, Junior had the family car and the credit card, credit having become a way of life by the time Junior could drive.

The draft had come suddenly for Daddy; for Junior it was the shadow hanging over his head from the time he learned to walk. The war that was going on when he began to approach draft age was one that not even the moralists were defending. While the major educative influence in his parents' home life (probably on a farm or in a small town) was their own parents, Junior's major educative influence, measured in hours spent, has been the television set and he has viewed it, most probably, in the context of a city with all the varied experiences of city life also available to him. Jet travel, immediate television relays from around the world and the reaches of outer space are taken for granted by the sons and daughters of persons who remember how many words were lost in static when Edward R. Murrow was reporting for CBS radio from a London rooftop during the blitz.

It ought to be no surprise, then, that the parent/child tension is so intense in our time. It is a tension on superficial as well as fundamental levels. Parents get uptight about long hair on boys, and neither the boys nor the girls can understand why their parents think of hair in sexual terms. Parents make bestsellers of *Portnoy's Complaint* and *Myra Breckinridge* and "for a lark" go to a topless joint; but they are upset if their children find nothing salacious in the nudity of *Hair*. Parents who recall the days of making home-brew and bathtub gin and fondly point out sites of the city's speak-easies of their past, find themselves confronting youngsters who, over the dinner table, argue for the legalization of pot.

More than this, however, parents find themselves on the spot as representing the established order that youngsters are now questioning. They find themselves challenged on the level of principle and ideals and living up to one's professed code by their own children. Some parents crack, overreact, seal themselves off from communication about anything that matters, or throw their children out as ingrates. Franciscan Father Simon Scanlon, whose ministry is in one of the vice centers of America, discusses what happens to some of these who have not found community at home.

The majority of today's young people have not been subjected to the silent treatment in regard to sexual matters. Better informed at an earlier age than their parents, not filled with misinformation and horror stories about disease (though venereal disease is now epidemic), they live in a time of sexual permissiveness and are subject to an ever-increasing amount of sexually stimulating material in movies, books, advertisements, and magazines. This, joined with the ready availability of the Pill, has fostered an almost precociously early sexual experimentation. Many of their peers are living together without marriage vows. The example given by persons they admire in the arts and entertainment fields of the same thing—including having children out of wedlock—they cite as evidence of the social acceptability of this. Some argue that society and the Church have no right to try to institutionalize their sexual love-making.

It is not to be wondered, then, that many parents—perhaps especially those who have honestly done their best to educate their children to independent use of their judgment and will—are finding themselves beleaguered, assailed by doubts and questions. Even for those whose children have not yet reached this stage of maturity, there are large questions concerning what the society holds in store for their lovely hostages of the future.

In what kind of society will my children be living? Am I of the last generation of parents to be free to have a family through personal decision? Social engineers and some medical men have already begun urging the goal of enforced family planning, of abortions without the consent of the father, of positive (as distinct from negative, i.e., "pulling the plug") euthanasia. The never-ending Asian war, the prospects of fascism at home, of nuclear war internationally, the knowledge that every new baby born has Strontium 90 in his bones and DDT in his fatty tissue, the running sores of our social maladies, also feed the fears held by parents for the future of their children.

These fears, seldom credible to the adolescent, are never far from thoughtful parents' consideration of their children's welfare. The realization that our youngsters are in many ways perhaps better equipped to handle that future than we ourselves are is of some solace, but part of that equipment must come from the parents. This burden is something drastically more psychologically demanding, and emotionally and physically exhausting than the work of parenthood was for our grandparents. It places upon the family a further load in addition to those named and others that the contributors to this volume discuss.

Strangely enough, few in our society seem at all aware that anything is happening *to* the family. This is one of the more puzzling aspects of the family life situation in our times—that the family seems to get only one of two kinds of treatment, neither of them helpful. The family is either ignored entirely when we are engaged in discussing what is going on in our world, or it is blamed for what is going on.

Most of us at one time or another have heard the family blamed for: juvenile crime, which has never been greater; drug addiction, which has never been greater; the illegitimacy rate, which has never been greater; racism; school dropouts; and student uprisings. For nearly every social ill we have, someone has pointed the accusing finger at the family, and at parents in particular.

When the family is not being blamed, it is ignored. Perhaps the best example I can offer of this is the personal experience of attendance at two regional White House conferences during the Kennedy administration. One of these was on the problems of America's youth. Reports and analyses were given of school dropout increases, juvenile crime, drug addiction, unemployment. Administration proposals for dealing with these matters were discussed; halfway houses, the Job Corps, the role of industry and school systems and juvenile authorities were considered. Yet in that full day of lectures, panels, and floor discussions, it was never once suggested that the youths being discussed might be members of families. That a particular youth's problems might be seen as part of his family's need, or that the problems of today might be fruitfully examined as an aspect of the crisis of family life in general, were simply ideas not to be entertained.

The same was true of another conference, this one on the country's aged. Not once was it suggested that the aged might be members of families and that it might be helpful to see what corrective help could be applied to a societal situation that cuts old people off from their families. Instead, insurance, convalescent homes, medical care, and housing projects for "senior citizens" received all the attention.

The basic misconception many seem to have about the family is that it is some sort of static entity. Most seem to assume that the family, like a redwood tree, grows older, adds another ring, but does not change very much in essence. It is for this reason that I have sought to give some hint of the prodigious changes that have come about in only the past few generations regarding our family life. Even so brief a sketch should demonstrate that the family is very much affected by what is happening in the world around it. In their various ways, the contributors to this volume leave no doubt that even more radical changes are going to come about in the years ahead.

We are, as Eulah Laucks indicates, in a period of history when the family is very much in transition. Mrs. Laucks accepts the fact that "part of the bridge to any future rests in the past," and moves from there to consider the transitional forms through which the family might create itself anew for a new age. The Birds offer the insight that part of our transition has been from a contractual concept of marriage to a relational one. William Bishop discusses some of the ways in which our marriage relationships have been influenced by our technologically oriented thinking. He cites some sources of the family of the future he discerns in our midst, including a new spirit of fidelity. Janet Golden explores fidelity as it relates to women presently re-evaluating their roles in marriage and society. Her comments should prove most helpful to those who believe that the search for personal fulfillment must run counter to faithfulness to the family.

One of the truths that even the most casual reader of this volume will not be able to avoid is that the family cannot be confined to some sort of traditional box, however crusted with historical mementoes and of however much sentimental value.

The historical functions of the family have been, for the most part, pried away from the family. The economic necessity for marriage is no longer there. The educational role of the family, in the main, has been taken over by the state and the media. Given the present sexual permissiveness in our society, marriage appears unnecessary for the satisfaction of sexual desires or the expression of physical love. I have had high school youths ask me, in all sincerity, "Why bother getting married?" College youths say, "We don't want to live in an institution," or "We love each other, we don't need any 'bonds of matrimony' to tie us together." Even the function of replenishing the race will soon, if population control enthusiasts prevail, become an offense punishable by taxation, or worse.

Such facts give almost spontaneous rise to the question: Can the family survive? Most of the contributors to this volume not only respond in the affirmative, they give reasons why the family is irreplaceable as the basic unit of society. The radical irreplaceability of the family to which these authors attest, writing from various disciplines, assures it of survival. The form that the family of the future will take will depend greatly upon the awareness of those now entering marriage and those who are rearing the founders of future families.

Sidney Callahan offers the invitation to us to extend our understanding of the whole concept of family, offering a vision of the future of the family from this point in its history when "we may be seeing just the beginning of the ascendance of the family as a self-conscious organism." Rosemary Haughton, looking toward the new kind of family we might be developing, not only reminds us that

Christians are meant to be different, but that the difference of the Christian family ought to be leading the way, as in the past, for all families into that future. Accepting this, Philip and Sally Scharper extrapolate from some present circumstances and trends to present a mind-expanding scan of some of the possible futures of the family.

The family does not exist in the abstract, save for the purposes of discussion. As every human person is unique, so is every marriage of two persons a unique marriage, and the family life that grows out of that marriage will likewise be unique. The substance of that family life is the interplay of all these personalities upon each other and their responses, individually and as a family, to the world about them.

Crucial to the sickness or health of any family, however, is the degree of commitment of the will that the various members—husband, wife, and children—bring to the task of building up one another in love. There is no better definition of the family than that it is a community of faithful lovers.

If that community of love is not to become a victim of the divorcing society, the generation gap, or the myriad fears and sicknesses of our time, its members must be conscious of what is happening around, about and to them as individuals and as a family. Out of that consciousness and their sensitivity to one another's needs can come the necessary judgments, adjustments, and responses that will lead to an increase, rather than a deterioration, of the bond of community.

However much we are products of history, however much our institutions are products of history, however much we and our families are caught up in the tensions and pressures of the present, we are always creating by our present choices and responses the future for ourselves and our families.

FUTURE OF THE FAMILY

MARRIAGE: A DOUBTFUL FUTURE

1

Joseph and Lois Bird

A pocket-sized crystal ball suitable for mounting on a typewriter stand and a box of instant tea leaves are indispensable tools to those who write for publication.

Push-button clairvoyance comes in handy when one is faced with questions on "The Future of Our Schools," "Fashions in the Twenty-first Century," or "Can the Family Survive?"

Sad to say, we have no sociological ouija board to spell out a word picture of marriage in, say, the last quarter of this century. The best we can do is to look at what has happened during the last fifty to seventy-five years, what seems to be going on today, and what we see as possible directions in the future, provided man permits himself a future.

In what has been called, among other things, the "agrarian society" of our grandparents or great-grandparents, to be left by the wayside unmarried was a social and economic tragedy. Marriage

1

was well-nigh a necessity. There were few jobs for women above the sweatshop or domestic level; they were educated for little else, and the few who were, found most doors closed to them. It therefore came down to a single course of action: find a husband. She needed a man to care for her, provide her with a home, food, clothing, and protection against what was often a hostile or exploitative world.

But nearly as much, a man needed a wife. While he cleared the land and worked the soil, he looked to her to cook his meals, sew his clothes, keep his house, and bear him sons who could take their place beside him in the fields.

Their marriage was a *contract* in the most literal sense. It called for specific roles, rights, and obligations. Even the Church spoke, quite dispassionately, of the "wifely duty" and the "rights of the husband." Both knew what to expect and what was expected of them, and so long as each lived up to the letter of the contract, it was considered to be a good marriage. The good husband worked hard, stayed sober, and refrained from beating his wife too severely or too frequently. For her part, the good wife kept a clean house, set a hearty table, and curbed a nagging tongue. And both were chaste. The contract was all simple enough. They could not reasonably ask for more—and they probably didn't.

Today's much discussed problems were probably nonexistent in these marriages. It is hard to believe they suffered from a lack of communication; they just did not have the time to communicate, not with the hours they worked. We doubt they were plagued by problems of *roles* and *identities*. They each knew who and what they were and what they were called upon to do, and that was that.

More important, however, is the fact that they each were aware of their obvious need for each other and for what can aptly be called a contractual marriage.

With urbanization, this all changed. The physical need structure of the contractual marriage disappeared. Women were no longer at the mercy of a masculine economy. In increasing numbers, women were educated for jobs. Today, there are few men working at occupations that have not been invaded by women. Few girls graduating from high school and college this year will marry as a means of economic survival. A man presently has no more material need for a wife than she does for a husband. He can somehow manage to clean his bachelor apartment without the aid of a wife, and even the poorest cook can struggle through preparation of a TV dinner. Nor does the modern male look on a future wife's childbearing potential as an economic asset; he docs not need sons to work the farm.

We still, nevertheless, talk about *needs*. They are now *emotional* needs that we seek to satisfy through marriage. These needs may be healthy or neurotic, mature or immature. Generally, they are a mixture of all. Hence, many answers could be given to the question, what does the contemporary man seek in marriage, and for what is his wife looking? Risking oversimplification, we contend that most are attempting to structure *cohabitive* relationships, while a minority are trying to attain what we have called *relational* marriages. Both models vary greatly from the contractual, as well as from each other.

In the *cohabitive* marriage, the spouses seek a relationship in which they can compatibly play out stereotypic social roles and satisfy physical needs. The reasons they give for marrying each other are generally that "everybody does" and "we fell in love." But they cannot define love, and they have never considered the whys and wherefores of the vocation they are supposedly entering for life. What they look for in selection of a mate differs little from what one might seek in a roommate, with a spun-sugar romantic love tossed in along with sex. They talk of "sharing interests," "working things out" (compromise, but not a gift of self), and, hopefully, "finding happiness." They find little meaning in their existence; they view life as something which happens to them, but over which they have little or no control, and they see themselves as a mere collection of social roles superimposed upon physical drives.

These marriages are every bit as much contracts—a set of stipulated rights and obligations—as were the *contractual* marriages, but with two important differences: The needs, and the rights and duties which relate to them, are psychosocial rather than material; and, the "terms" of the contract are vastly more ambiguous; they are seldom sure what they should or should not agree upon.

Their goals center on being friends and lovers, and they speak in the words of a vague personalism. The key to the relationship is *sharing*. Their lives remain distinct; "oneness" is a concept which has no place in the *cohabitive* marriage. He has his job, his interests, his friends, and his masculine world; she has a world of her own. There are also areas of overlap. These, they *share*. They may share an interest in golf, politics, religion, and vodka gimlets. In the same fashion, they share a ranch-style house in the suburbs and three children, but it seldom goes much deeper. They just happen, quite by chance, to like some of the same things or bear some of the same responsibiilties (over which they may bicker). In those areas in which they have no common interest, they go their separate ways. He builds a life of sorts around career, golf game, and television set. She shapes hers around the coffee klatch, parish, children, and television set. If one were to ask, they might even say theirs is a happy marriage. Why not? It is probably no less happy than those of most of their friends. They, too, have *cohabitive* marriages.

Then there is the *relational* marriage. Here, the primary and overriding emphasis is on the relationship itself. The spouses may, and in time no doubt will, share as many or more interests and activities as their cohabiting friends, but their sights are set not on merely collecting shared involvements and hobbies, but on attaining a single identity which is a blend of the complementary identities of each: *"That two shall become one."* These marriages develop out of the most intense personal encounters and the most self-revealing communication. The spouses strive to enter one another's worlds; they work to lower any and all boundaries which separate them. It is their total relationship which transcends all other values, persons, and interests. They do not live in an ivory tower, but they step out of their tower *hand in hand*.

The *relational* marriage demands a great deal of time and effort, as well as heroic courage. The growth process may be very painful. Many men and women have simply not reached the level of maturity necessary for such a relationship. Perhaps, given enough time, they could, but why not stick with a *cohabitive* marriage and avoid the painful exposure? Why not indeed? This, of course, is what so many choose to do. And they go blissfully along, feeling little pain, in a pleasant companionship, with sex as an added bonus. They may even remain in this limbo of *McCall's* "togetherness" so long as one of two eventualities does not occur: situations which demand immediate and intense communication (for which they are unprepared), or, an attempt on the part of one to restructure the relationship toward a *relational* marriage. This latter usually is motivated by a growing awareness of meaninglessness, the feeling that "there must be more to life than this," so pervasive today. The partner in such a marriage may react to the attempted restructuring with, "Hey, that's no fair; you're trying to change the rules." And he is right. What he bargained for was the safe distance of a cohabitive marriage; now he finds that his spouse wants to be closer. Understandably, he rebels.

So long as the cohabitive marriage goes along pretty smoothly and each has sufficient distractions, there may be no breakdown. Children often provide the primary distraction for the wife, and they provide conversational material which passes for communication. But these couples may actually fear the coming day when the children will be gone. They may try to prolong the distraction and involvement through grandchildren (and, in doing so, painfully disrupt the next generation). The garden club sages will tell them to find hobbies and outside involvements to "fill the gap," but seldom are these attempts to sustain a painless *cohabitive* marriage enough; their world becomes, increasingly, an egocentric void of loneliness.

Since these constitute the majority, we may now look to the future and ask whether marriage, as we know it, will survive. It seems unlikely.

The twenty-hour work week and the thirteen-week annual vacation have been predicted. We have far more leisure time than did our parents; our children will have still more. Many responsible social scientists view this as a source of major psychological and social problems. After all, the bowling leagues, garden clubs, parish organizations, and cocktail lounges must have finite limits. At some point, then, couples will be faced with nothing to fill the void other than themselves. Some have already discovered what can happen. They either sit in silence or stumble over words, and they get hurt. When they cannot talk, the aching silence builds like a throbbing tooth; when they try to communicate, they hit nerves. They may go out for an evening, but they play it safe and take along another couple. If they stay home, they retreat into a television set. With a future promising more free time, those with cohabitive marriages will go still further down separate paths and structure their relationships even more as "living arrangements."

One other variable is important in predicting this future: children. The main shared interest of most couples seems to be, as we have said, their offspring. The children not only provide a distraction that saves the couple from a painful confrontation, they also furnish husband and wife with whatever meaning they find in their relationship. What of the next generation? We can expect many, moved by concern for a world in hunger or caught in the fallout of SRO cities, to either remain childless or limit their progeny to one or two. What form will their marriages take?

Cohabitive marriages may become the norm, not by default or a failure to achieve something more, but by intent and agreement. If so, the involvements will be even less intense than those we presently see; they will be, by choice, living arrangements, with the pair going their separate ways much of the time. With fewer mutual responsibilities, these marriages, we can expect, will have less permanence. As their goals and interests change, so will their choice of mates.

This is not a prediction so much as a logical extrapolation, an inescapable conclusion if we plot today's cohabitive marriage along a time line into tomorrow. With nothing to intervene to reshape the ways in which the sexes interact, they will follow the course, neurotic and depersonalized though it may be, that we have charted, and the present ideal of marriage and the family—to which we often pay less than lip service—will indeed join the buffalo and buggy whip, to be replaced by transitory and superficial "arrangements."

Can *relational* marriages emerge? Perhaps. If, and this is a very big *if,* the world of 1990 is populated by men and women who have attained a maturity and an emotional and intellectual freedom that will permit a vocational choice structured on values that transcend the mere expedient and socially sanctioned, the *relational* marriage may "come into its own" and may become a reality of the "oneness" which has heretofore been too often viewed as a naive theological abstraction.

The wise social scientist does not write of what he ideally hopes the future may be. Such rhetoric is left to the politicians and in-spirational preachers. He observes, he studies, he notes existing con-ditions and correlative events, and he then predicts. At most, he may suggest what seem to be alternative choices in behavior. He is neither a moralist nor a prophet. In our Age of Aquarius, predic-tion has become increasingly difficult. The written word has an em-barrassing permanence and the writer, if he is to maintain an intel-lectual vitality, is forced to continually re-examine that which he has written only a year or two ago and, all too frequently, reject it in the light of more recent trends and events.

What would we say of the direction of marriage today? Certainly not what we were saying ten years ago, nor even five years ago. The world in which we live is not the world of five years ago and only the man blinded by fear and a reactive resistance to change would argue that things are pretty much as they always were and that "the kids were doing and saying the same things in my day." It is a "brand new day," a new world in which the cultural patterns of an earlier age simply no longer seem applicable or acceptable. It may be tempting to think in terms of some sort of "eternal veri-ties" and unchangeable laws and institutions, but if we are to con-tinue to *live* in the world and work to change it to something better, we must recognize those inevitable changes, the developments which have brought them about, and the ultimate results which can be predicted from them.

In the last quarter century we have witnessed a technological revolution far more dramatic, much more rapid and sweeping, and with greater predictable consequences than the industrial revolution. Significant events have followed significant events at a speed which has telescoped time. A recap of the news stories of the 1960's takes on the appearance of a recap of a half century. And as with previous periods in which dramatic changes in technology have taken place, all existing institutions have been brought into question in the last two decades. Most are now under siege. Relevancy has become the question, and the familiar basis of an indictment. Our churches, educational establishments, governments, monetary systems, ethics, moralities, and societal structures are being torn open and torn down. The institutions of marriage and the family are not being spared. Any and all of our existing institutions may fall under the weight of the fast-moving social juggernaut being towed by a speeding technology.

We may shed a nostalgic tear, but we cannot afford the luxury of living in the past, of following leaders who offer the temporary comfort of a status quo built on shifting sands. We must recognize that the wisdom of the ages—and the wisdom of the aged—had its most significant application and made its greatest contribution during the age in which it was contemporary. Its value to us is to be found only in its relevance to our present age, and only in the areas in which the pertinent circumstances are relatively the same. The leaders—educational, religious, and political—who speak of the "good old days" and counsel us to resist change rather than seek innovation are less foolish than dangerous. They captain a ship of fools sailing toward a reef of anarchy. The ship's saloon may offer comfort and even a quaint charm. Taking to the lifeboats may indeed be frightening. But abandoning the ship and facing the choppy waters with only a vaguely charted course may be our only chance for survival.

Indeed, these are harsh alternatives to face. The prospect of change, when it implies change to the unknown, is always most difficult to accept. Hitler spoke of a Reich which would last for a thousand years, and the German people wanted to believe it and many did. We take comfort in the permanence of a republic which has survived for 200 years, and will last forever? Or a Church with a history of 2000 years ordained until the end of time? Monogamous marriage, we say, antedates recorded history. As an institution, it will always be with us. But will it?

The young, in increasing numbers, are saying, no. They have looked at the marriages of their parents; they have watched the marriage situation comedies on television; they have been taught to have their fun while they are single since marriage is "no bed of roses." And they have asked, "Who needs it?" Try to recall when you last read a love story or viewed a romantic movie in which the principal characters were husband and wife. The kids look at marriage as presented by the establishment and they turn their backs on what they see. We call them "romantics" and "idealists" as if the labels were dirty words. Is it because we have killed romance in our own lives and lost what idealism we once may have had? Have we accepted dead, mechanistic relationships as inevitable, and marriage as the least dynamic of all, with its survival being its only viable goal? What model do we give our children? Try to picture Dick and Pat making love by moonlight on a deserted beach!

What the changes in technology have brought about are reflected in the rejections voiced by youth, and they are most vocal in their rejection of legalism and absolutes. To say, "It won't happen," or "We won't permit it to happen" is to risk even more dire consequences than we may anticipate. The legalism of the marriage contract and the model of the institution of marriage with all its traditional *rights* and *obligations* will most surely cease to exist because, as the parents of today's youth have shown in their own relationships, it no longer has an appeal. *Love* does have an appeal. The ability to love and be loved is, in fact, as necessary to our emotional survival as food and drink are to our physical survival. But love in the relationship is not built upon a framework of legalism and social convention. The mature marriage of a man and woman is founded on mutual love, a day-by-day choice of living together in mutual giving of self. The love did not arise out of a contract, nor is it strengthened by a contract. Existence of the contract may even contribute to a lessening of love in the relationship.

How is this so? It comes about because we are all subject to the influence of our associations to the words we employ and the concepts they represent. The words *marriage, husband, wife,* and *family* all trigger associations learned early and reinforced by our personal experience. By the time we reached adulthood, they may have formed themselves into stereotypes of convention. The stereotypes may be less than healthy, but they are not easily broken. We have learned marriage is a "binding" contract, often a rut, and in some cases a "cross." New youth, fearing neither the social rejection nor eternal hellfire that influenced our acceptance of the marriage norm, are turning their backs on the *institution* of marriage and all the stoic acceptance of the inevitable it implies.

Then will marriage cease to exist? All the existing evidence would seem to indicate that it will. At least, marriage as we have known it. Will we then see couples living in nothing but transitory and superficial "arrangements"? Perhaps. It may depend upon whether they are offered an attractive, viable alternative. If they witness couples, especially their parents, living in relationships founded on love rather than legalism, relationships which have a permanence because they are continually growing while at the same time freely chosen at all times, they may choose to emulate them. These will be the relational marriages.

Will they be the marriages of the future? Realistically, we cannot be optimistic. The challenge of the future is here today and has partially passed us by. It demands a true revolution, an almost overnight leap into responsible adulthood. Such marriages can be developed only by thinking men and women, capable of building meaningful values for themselves, and courageous enough to battle upstream toward an ideal; adults who are not looking to the external criteria of what their society dictates for their relationship, nor to the legal games of validity or invalidity of their contract.

Lacking an appropriate model, there seems little chance that the following generations of adults will strive to build such mature relationships. We live in the "institution" they so often view with disdain. In the future they will see our marriages as unions of love, truly *relational* marriages, or as restrictive cohabitive contracts. And if they see only the latter, we will join them in asking, "Who needs it?"

WILL THE FAMILY SURVIVE THE TWENTIETH CENTURY?

2

Joan Bel Geddes

More and more often these days, you hear the daring (or despairing) remark, "Marriage is obsolete—the family is a dying institution!" Various serious social ills—slums, racial tension, crime, drug addiction, mental illness—are seen as causes or results of unhappy, inadequate family life. The startling changes in morals and manners in our century are regarded by many people as proof that the family no longer provides an emotionally healthy environment for the young, and sound or consistent moral guidance.

Before diagnosing something as dying, one should have a clear idea of what it is like when it is thriving. But do we know exactly what the family is like? Sociologists, anthropologists and the Church all say the family is "the basic unit of society," the most fundamental of all social institutions. We are all familiar *(sic)* with it in daily life. Yet it eludes definition. (This is not surprising. Everything really important defies glib, precise definition. Males and females argue endlessly over what femininity or masculinity is, and probably always will. Artists cannot agree on what Art is. Who can neatly define Beauty? Love? Or God?)

Most people assume that the type of family they know is the norm. Whether they are attacking or defending it they think *the* family's reputation is at stake. The family, however, can and does exist in many forms. It may be patriarchal or matriarchal or a combination; monogamous or polygamous; an unsupported "nuclear" family or an extended family. Within these forms there are many variations. Rules about consanguinity, mutual consent, marital roles, age of partners, betrothal practices, child care procedures and child behavior, inheritance laws, as well as etiquette, social customs, and economic factors that intimately affect family life, vary much more than most people realize, according to personal tastes, class, culture, geography, and epoch.

For example, the father is the head of the family in some societies, and many Catholics assume that this is part of "the natural law." Yet in other societies this honor, and the responsibilities attached to it, belongs to the mother or the grandmother or grandfather or eldest uncle or aunt. One recent psychological study indicates that in some respects having the mother as the family head might be more natural than our arrangement, because children raised in a matriarchal family showed more stability and better emotional adjustment, and had fewer behavior problems (but less initiative) than other children.

We think of child marriage as a Hindu practice, yet in Elizabethan England many children married at nine or ten, and in eleven Latin American countries, all officially Catholic, it is legal for girls of twelve to marry.

We think of marriage arranged by parents as an Oriental institution, yet this was normal procedure in Europe until the nineteenth century. Many babies had their mates selected for them as soon as they were born . . . like being enrolled in a good school at birth. The Church now teaches that marriages performed without the free and full consent of both partners are invalid, but it officially sanctioned marriage by capture until the ninth century, and even until the nineteenth century in parts of eastern Europe where both Orthodox and

Roman Catholic boys customarily obtained wives by forcible abduction.

We deplore the "bride price" customary among African tribes, but until recently the dowry was an accepted aspect of Christian marriage and is still required of "brides of Christ" in some religious orders.

We think of premarital sex as illicit, yet in the "ages of faith" it was usual for engaged couples to have sexual relations. A mother living in North America may be horrified if her teen-age daughter sleeps with several boys, but a mother living in the South Pacific may be quite distressed if her teen-age daughter does not, because she considers such activity useful practice for being happily married, like learning how to cook before the wedding day. We may call her attitude immoral but she would consider ours an irrational, unrealistic, and even harmful taboo. St. Thomas More didn't go as far as she does but he certainly went farther than we do when he insisted that William Roper see Margaret and her sister naked before proposing to Margaret, on the grounds that one should not buy anything without looking it over carefully first.

We think of plural wives as Moslem or pagan, but many a Christian king had an official and a morganatic wife simultaneously and raised both wives' children in one household, and in the era of Christian knighthood it was considered quite proper to have a strong romantic attachment to someone else's spouse.

We may disapprove of the selfishness and hedonism of men in ancient Greece as described by Demosthenes when he said, "We keep mistresses for pleasure, concubines for daily attendance upon our persons, and wives to bear us legitimate children and be our housekeepers," but in Catholic Spain, among many of the "best families," it is common for a man's wife to attend to his children and home while less ladylike ladies attend to his recreational and sexual appetites. In Catholic France having mistresses in coexistence with wives has long been regarded as normal and sensible, and in England, between the pubs and clubs and model agencies, many conventionally "good husbands" spend most of their leisure time away from their families.

Catholics frequently point the finger of disapproval at Scandinavia because of the large number of unmarried mothers there, but in Catholic South America having an illegitimate child does not shock people as much as it does in Protestant North America, and in fact, Latin America has the highest illegitimate birth rate of any region in the world. Also, during the centuries when all Europe was Catholic, being born out of wedlock did not stigmatize a person as much as it does today in some post-Christian cultures.

Educated Catholics realize that theirs is not the only valid form of family life; they know God was not angry with Abraham and Sarah when they agreed he should take a concubine in order to produce an heir. Nonetheless, over the centuries, the Catholic family has acquired certain typical features. They used to be characteristic of most families in the Western world, but because Catholic mores (for better and for worse) change more slowly than those of people unconcerned about preserving any inherited institutions and values, they have come to seem uniquely Catholic in recent decades: rarity of divorce; swarms of children; authoritarian husbands and fathers; and docile stay-at-home wives.*

How did the kind of family we now think of as typical—patriarchal, nuclear, monogamous—develop, and why did it become predominant in Christendom? We inherited it from pagan Rome, not because it was the only, or best, or ideal form of family, but because Rome is where Christianity first joined "the Establishment." Ethnic and class characteristics have a way of becoming fused and confused with religious ideals, though they are merely one of several possible ways of trying to incarnate those ideals.

The evolving Christian society adopted and adapted many cultural features of its Roman milieu and abandoned some that still characterize life in the Eastern Mediterranean where Christianity was born.

The Roman family was far from ideal. The father had a tyrant's power *(pater potestas)* over all other members to a degree that everyone today would consider intolerable. He had literal rights of life

---

* I refuse to call them "nonworking wives" because those who do homework often work much harder than those who escape from the kitchen into an office. I also dislike the term "housewives" because a woman's husband should be a man not a house, Demosthenes notwithstanding.

and death over his children, whom he could legally have killed for disobedience—even when they were grown up—and who could be, and frequently were, killed at birth simply because he did not want them. I once saw a copy of an interesting letter from a Roman soldier to his pregnant wife. It is a chatty, affectionate, charming letter, tenderly solicitous of her health, but it ends with a reminder that if the baby is a girl she must not forget to have the midwife kill it.

The Roman wife had no property rights and no rights over her own children. She was expected to stay home all the time, not just some of the time. After the age of four or five her boys were taken away from her, to live in a separate part of the house so that they would escape softening feminine influence. She had nothing to say about their education.

The Roman family was not even very stable. People who worry about how the modern family is disintegrating might cheer themselves by comparing today's divorce rates with those of ancient Rome. Although, according to the laws instituted by Romulus, a wife could not divorce her husband no matter how cruel or neglectful he might be, the husband could divorce her if she committed adultery, poisoned her children, or had a duplicate set made of his keys! In the last days of the Roman Republic, divorce by either spouse was permitted and *annual* divorces became the fashion in high society; Seneca said that there were women who reckoned their age by the number of husbands they had had.

Yet this type of father-dominated family endured, with modifications, through the centuries, perpetuated by Christian society—until recently when the ideal of a more democratic family structure, with shared authority, has gained many advocates. Within this family framework the Church has tried hard to teach morality, stressing those virtues that seemed most conducive to domestic peace: obedience, fidelity, prudence, patience, perseverance, chastity, and charity. Some Christians were, and are today, so convinced that charity begins at home that they let it end there. They love "their own" warmly and sincerely while dwelling in voluntarily erected physical and spiritual ghettos that exclude outsiders. Yet Christ said to love your neighbor as yourself, not your closest blood relatives.

Only one quality should characterize, always and everywhere, the

Christian family, or any Christian anything: *love*. "See those Christians, how they love one another!" Members of a Christian family should be distinguished for the depth, warmth, sincerity, and loyalty of their mutual devotion and for pace-setting hospitality and neighborliness. But alas, at their worst they tend to be just as quarrelsome, petty, materialistic, and selfish as other people and at their best their loveliness and lovingness are not specifically or exclusively Christian traits: "Do not even pagans love those who are good to them?"

Love is no one's monopoly. It is simply the essence of true goodness, though that fact is obscured nowadays, when the word "love" is used to describe so many things. To many, love means physical attraction, emotional titillation, or possessiveness. These may not always coexist with "willing the good of the other" as St. Thomas defined love. Most people today think of love as something extraordinary they may "fall in" if they are lucky, rather than as something normal they can themselves create and build, which has more to do with will than with luck.

Americans praise love and think that family love is exemplified by togetherness, but does our typically independent family, consisting of only one pair of parents and their young children, really demonstrate those qualities more than the extended family of Africa and Asia in which aunts, uncles, grandparents, cousins, nieces, and nephews are all included?

Even second and third cousins are in some family systems as close as, or closer than, sisters and brothers are in ours. In America many of us do not even know the names of our cousins or great-grandparents, let alone associate with them or look after them. We are so used to this that it does not seem strange or unnatural to us. What we consider distant relatives used to be so close that for centuries the Church forbade marriage even among fifth cousins because they were siblings (we only call brothers and sisters "siblings," but the word means members of the same "sib" or tribe, and it is because Jesus grew up in a culture where the extended family was the norm that he referred to his cousins as his brothers).

Many dropouts from home these days seem to be trying to reach beyond the narrow confines of the nuclear family unit, seeking (even in blind alleys) togetherness in a new type of extended family. They have found that when all one's emotional eggs are in one small basket, when love is based exclusively on biological and physical closeness, togetherness can become oppressive. Concern for a spouse's or child's welfare can degenerate into perpetual nagging, and mother love can turn into "smother love." As Kahil Gibran wrote, there must be "spaces in your togetherness . . . trees cannot grow in each other's shadow." (He also had something wise to say to parents about the generation gap: "Your children do not belong to you—they belong to tomorrow, a world you cannot enter.")

People in our type of family often become tense and hostile and resentful of or overdependent on each other, and as a result suffer psychological difficulties throughout their lives. Resentment of parents can overflow into hatred of all authority figures, to the detriment of society. In the post-Freudian era we have heard a lot about the lasting damage caused by an unresolved Oedipus or Electra complex.

One psychiatrist has observed that if Freud had been as interested in the Bible as he was in Greek literature he would also have written about "the Isaac complex." We know that "baby blues" are suffered by most young mothers and fathers because parenthood is so confining and demanding, especially in an unsupported nuclear family, and therefore causes emotional ambivalence. Many fathers may have an unconscious wish to get rid of their sons, for although a son is an extension of his father's ego and a source of pride he is also a threat to the father's dominance, since his destiny is to replace and even to surpass the father. According to this analysis, the angel that stayed Abraham's hand was a vision, or sudden flash of insight, whereby Abraham realized and fully accepted the idea that God wants a father to protect his son and does not want the son to be sacrificed by him, even when the father thinks he has a good reason. (Will the world's fathers ever get a similar revelation and stop sending their sons to be killed in wars, thinking they are justified in using them as necessary sacrifices to uphold their ideals?)

To escape spiritual claustrophobia, searching for bigger and better groups of people with whom to identify, teen-agers full of illusions and middle-agers full of disillusionment are leaving home today in increasing numbers. Their desertion of their loved ones shocks and distresses us, but are not at least some of them acting as Christ did when he wandered off with a group of friends and associated with sinners? He once refused, rather rudely, to see his mother and "brothers" when they came to visit him, saying "Who is my mother and who are my brothers?" and then, turning toward his new friends, said "Here are my mother and my brothers." He even said, "He who does not hate his mother and father for My sake is not worthy of Me." This is an extremely hard teaching for a mother or father to understand and accept, but it accords with the modern psychologists' observation that no one can be a mature and mentally healthy person until the spiritual umbilical cord is cut—and besides, who ever said that being a true Christian is easy?

Whether an action is virtuous or sinful depends in part on *why* it is done. If a youngster drops out of school or home to indulge himself lazily or destructively, he hurts his family and himself, but what if he does it to work hard and generously for McCarthy, Vista, the Peace Corps or some Mississippi sharecroppers? When he comes back home again he may bring new spiritual riches with him, and meantime he is growing. His concept of the family is widening, not diminishing, if he is taking seriously the idea that all mankind is one family. His departure need not be interpreted as desertion. In our mobile society you *can* go home again—by car, bus, train, or plane —unlike the days when sons left parents forever in the old country to seek adventure or prosperity in the new world (yet our country's founding fathers are not despised as dropouts who destroyed family life; instead of calling them disloyal deserters of their parents, we respectfully refer to them as brave pioneers, immigrants, colonists, or explorers).

In the parable of the Good Samaritan, Christ tried to teach us that anyone in need is our neighbor, and "Love your neighbor" is a commandment, the essence of God's holy law, not a counsel of perfection. In the parable of the lilies of the field, he tried to teach us not to overvalue material security. But most of us, both rich and poor, for two thousand years have neglected both of these lessons. Many youngsters have decided it is high time to start emphasizing these parts of Christ's message.

In concentrating with special fervor, in its traditional teachings, on the virtues of obedience and chastity, the Church has not been unique. "Honor your father and mother" is by no means exclusively a Christian idea. Jews and Moslems also believe at least officially in the Ten Commandments, and filial piety has been emphasized even more emphatically in Buddhist, Confucian and Shinto families than by Christianity. *The Precepts of Ptan-Hotep,* said to be the oldest book in existence (written in Egypt more than 3000 years before Christ) said, "Bring up your son in obedience . . . Obedience is beloved of God; disobedience is hated by God." And, as noted earlier, in pre-Christian Rome a father had the legal right to punish disobedience with death.

Yet the Church has canonized disobedient children. St. Francis of Assisi and St. Clare adamantly refused to obey their parents and deserted their respectable families for a life of dirt and poverty. Martin de Porres was a disobedient son when he gave to beggars the money his mother had given him to buy the family's food. Would-be nuns and priests have frequently defied parents unwilling to part with them. Many of today's youngsters who spurn family security or convention to go and work in antipoverty programs or the peace movement are acting in the same spirit of rebellion, not motivated so much by disobedience to their elders as by obedience to something that takes precedence: their own wide-awake consciences.

Are obedience, chastity, reverence, and loyalty real values and virtues? Does the lack of them threaten today's families? Yes, just as lack of other virtues harmed yesterday's families in different ways. Openness, flexibility, sincerity, generosity, compassion, freedom, honesty, initiative, and courage are real values, too. The trouble is that so few of us are capable of practicing *all* virtues, so we pick and choose, in practice if not in theory.

In our era, all over the world, the current overriding trend is toward expansion, mobility, and independence. Courage is admired more than prudence; spontaneity more than perseverance; truthfulness more than tact; sincerity more than good manners. People are turning the traditional priority list of virtues upside down and inside out. With Martin Luther King's heroic example shining like a light in the darkness caused by hatred among races, classes, and nations, some people are even deciding it is more important to "love your enemies" and "bless those who persecute you" than it is to "honor your father and mother."

Youngsters are turned off by sermons about honesty, kindness, love, and decency from people who are indifferent to the problems of the poor and blind to their own failings while terribly disturbed by those of other people (the old "mote in your brother's eye" problem). They dislike being taught "thou shalt not kill" by people who believe in killing—so they are turning their swords into paintbrushes and making colorful posters, buttons, and bumper stickers that proclaim "Make love not war." For them morality has left the bedroom to march on picket lines, and charity begins away from home.

Many youngsters so much hate the double-think of people who say one thing and do the opposite that they try to be honest at all costs. They refuse to make promises they may not be able to keep. This is why many of them cheerfully live together without the formality of marriage, not to abolish the family but to avoid that type of family where members stick together "loyally" while bickering and tormenting each other. There is a Russian proverb that says "No love is so ardent that it cannot be cooled down by marriage." Today's youngsters prefer the risks of insecurity and uncertainty to the risks of conventionality and security. They enjoy temporary relationships which, for the duration—however brief or long that may be—are warm and intimate. They do not feel that intimacy is something they must carefully avoid until they have a written guarantee that it will be permanent. In fact, having observed their elders, they are convinced that neither vows nor contracts can *guarantee* permanence, and this judgment can hardly be considered rash, since it is based on abundant evidence. It is the older generation's reliance on the lifelong magical result of signatures on pieces of paper that might be called rash, superstitious, and naive.

Does the unwillingness of some young couples to commit themselves to each other forever mean that from now on there will be few lifelong unions? If your answer is yes, you must be even more skeptical about the possibility of happy family life than today's younger generation, and seriously believe that few people ever love each other enough to stay together voluntarily. As Bernard Shaw once remarked, "Those who talk most about the blessings of marriage and the constancy of its vows are the very people who declare that if the chain were broken and the prisoners left free to choose, the whole social fabric would fly asunder. You cannot have the argument both ways. If the prisoner is happy, why lock him in? If he is not, why pretend that he is?"

Youngsters who say they love each other do not take a vow *not* to stay together. They simply say they do not know what the future holds, and therefore want to remain free and grant freedom to the person they love, though for the time being they feel strongly committed to each other. But does "commitment" really mean anything in that kind of open-ended relationship? Older people think commitment means the promise never to live in separate residences, but in the meantime, on a day-to-day basis, they may not be especially close, having many unshared interests, differing tastes, opinions, attitudes, and the like. They do not understand how people who have made no promises to each other can possibly call themselves committed. Yet the youngsters do not see how such lukewarm "lovers" as their parents are can possibly think they are committed to each other. In other words, what the young usually mean by the word "commitment" is an intense and wholehearted concern for the present despite agnosticism about the future; they wish to give *all* of themselves to each other "in truth and in deed" right now, even though they think it possible they will feel differently tomorrow. With them, as with St. Paul, "the acceptable time is *now.*"

It is futile to blame such attitudes on the heedlessness and shortsightedness of youth, even though it is true that by nature the young are more aware of what they want today than of their possible need for old-age security tomorrow. The sins of the fathers have been visited on the sons, and thanks to the huge stockpile of lethal weapons and the air, water, and land pollution their parents have produced, young people consider it urgent to live *now* as fully as possible because they are not sure how long they or the world will be here; there may not be any tomorrow.

Which type of couple is more sincerely and fully loving, the "faithful unto death" but long since bored-with-each-other couple, or the ardently devoted-for-the-time-being couple? This seems to me the type of judgment only God can make. Neither is perfectly committed; the ideal would be a combination of the loving aspects of both relationships. But how many human beings are capable of perfect love?

Parents would not be so worried and horrified by their children's temporary liaisons if they were platonic, but they are not. Extramarital and premarital sex have always been facts of life, of course, but never before so openly admitted and even advocated. This deeply shocks people who have always believed in a sexual double standard, the theory that it does not matter so much what you do as long as you keep quiet about it and do not get caught, and the puritan notion that loss of virginity is a fate worse than death for an unmarried girl.

Everyone is in large part a product of cultural conditioning, having absorbed unconsciously many ideas and attitudes by social osmosis rather than arriving at them by clear objective thinking and free choice. African tribes are by no means the only groups that follow sacred taboos, and many an American grandmother is as irrationally appalled at seeing her grandson wear love beads and shoulder-length hair as an African grandmother is at seeing her granddaughter eat eggs.*

Perhaps when we are deeply shocked by sexual freedom we are truly feeling God-given moral indignation, or perhaps we are secretly envious that we never had the freedom and courage to experience such openly expressed joy (I'm not saying we are; I'm just speculating). But as St. Paul said, it does not really matter what other people think of one's behavior, not even what we think of our own; what does matter is what God thinks of it. All any of us can do is try to do what we think is right (while realizing with humility that *perfect* behavior is beyond our power and that we must forgive ourselves and others for occasional inevitable lapses), and hope that our opinion coincides with God's while having enough generosity to allow for the possibility that the other person's may.

* Salutary thought for parents of long-haired sons: In Rome's ancient days long hair was a sign of aristocracy or nobility; only "barbarians" wore their hair short . . . and to cut the hair of a boy or girl against their will in medieval France meant a fine of 45 sous.

Did Christ himself condemn sex among unmarried people? He certainly condemned adultery, which is illicit sex among married people. But he recommended forgiveness of it ("Let whoever is without sin cast the first stone") and he did not condemn any sexual misbehavior as sternly or as frequently as he condemned pride and hypocrisy and money-changing in the temple; in short, the sins of "the Establishment." These are the very sins that young people today also most strongly condemn, while most older people tend to think they do not matter terribly, or are inevitable, or are not there. So can we be confident that our more "mature" value judgments are more Christian than, or even as Christian as, our children's value judgments? ("Not all who call me Lord do the will of My Father.")

Our traditional attitudes used to seem like Absolute Truth to us, but we have learned that many things we used to consider absolutely true are not. We have come to realize that it is more Christian to concern ourselves with our neighbors' needs and rights than to make lengthy novenas trying to save our own souls in isolation. It is hard now to look back and understand how we could ever have believed some of the things we were certain of a few years ago.

For centuries morality has been taught by people belonging to a special class that was required, for both spiritual and practical reasons, to be celibate. They had more education than the average person could obtain in the preprinting press world, and they were often wise, kind, and admirable people, but like all human beings they had limitations, and therefore "saw through a glass darkly." They had a vested interest, too, in persuading us (and themselves) that enforced chastity is holier than freedom. St. Peter's successor today holds firmly to the traditional reverence for celibacy (despite the fact that St. Peter was married), but he is forced to recognize that a great many people disagree with him.

Only in recent years has the Church enthusiastically praised sex as a good thing even within marriage, although God invented sex. Read St. Jerome and other Fathers of the Church if you think its current teachings about the holiness of marriage are part of an unchanging tradition. St. Jerome wrote: "He who too ardently loves his own wife is an adulterer." The Manichean prejudice against the physical expression of love prevailed as late as the twelfth century in official Church writings. In the seventh century a married couple had to abstain from cohabitation for three nights before they could receive communion. In the memory of people still alive, many nuns and monks considered it sinful even to look at one's own naked body, let alone that of someone else.

Does this inconsistency mean we must either sneer at past viewpoints or fear present ones? No. All living things grow, including the Church, and growth always involves change. People have new experiences and as a result learn new things. As long as we live we face the continuing necessity for adjustments and readjustments.

The word "free" and the word "love" both represent ideals we claim to cherish, yet most of us think that as soon as they are combined into one phrase, free love, they mean lascivious irresponsibility. So-called free thinkers deny this. For example, Bertrand Russell, one of the most notorious advocates of free love, was respectful of enduring attachments. In his book *Marriage and Morals* he wrote, "Most wholesomely constituted people desire, and will continue to desire, to have children; they will go on feeling that the best guardians of children are their parents living together in a permanent union. And when we put aside the question of children . . . and consider only the facts of personality, a permanent union is still required for development. In a series of transitory unions no two people can really ever know each other and all the possibilities each holds; they only take the first step on a road which beyond all others leads to the heart of life." And in another passage: "Moreover, the view that romantic love is essential to marriage is too anarchic, and . . . forgets that children are what make marriage important. But for children, there would be no need of any institution concerned with sex, but as soon as children enter in, the husband and wife, if they have any sense of responsibility or any affection for their offspring, are compelled to realize that their feelings toward each other are no longer what is of most importance."

Except for the first part of the last sentence, that sounds quite conventional (Russell held that it is the birth of the first child, not the first act of sexual intercourse, that consummates a marriage and makes it binding). This advanced thinker now seems a bit old-fashioned, at least in these passages, for people have recently begun to realize that even the idea that parents should stay together "for the sake of the children" is not always true.

Do the needs of children take precedence over those of adult members of a family? Most Americans would say yes. Why? Because children are by nature incapable of meeting their own needs and depend on others for survival. Yet children used to have to adapt willy-nilly to their parents' wishes and needs rather than the other way around. If our ancestors saw the way we worry about childhood traumas, and the extent to which we rearrange our habits and schedules for the convenience and pleasure of our children, they would be astounded, and disapproving. In the past, whereas it was unthinkable for a wife not to attend eagerly to all her husband's needs and demands and wishes, it was quite thinkable for a mother to spend very little time waiting on her children; today things are reversed—one more example of the variability of value judgments regarding human relationships.

In our time we have discovered that a good home can be provided for children without two parents. Adoption agencies now allow single people to adopt, not merely as a lesser evil but because they have seen that in certain cases it can be highly desirable. There is something else we have seen too, much to our sorrow and even horror. Parents are *not* always the best people to take care of children. Witness the chilling statistics about child abuse, that great skeleton in the human family's closet which few have had the courage to look at in all its shattering ugliness. It is the cause of more deaths among children than most major diseases, but we cannot bear to think that anyone can really be so unnatural as to harm consciously and seriously his or her own child. Unfortunately, unnaturalness is a lot more natural than we care to admit, and sentimental or spiritual generalizations about the sacredness of mother love or the necessity of permanent family ties cannot bring back to life the many helpless babies who have been beaten or starved to death by sick, unhappy, or vicious parents.

Although the desire for a permanent union with people one loves is as instinctive in normal people as the desire to care for one's children, even the Church—by permitting separation—acknowledges that this universally desired ideal is sometimes difficult or impossible to achieve. In many cases it may be better, in order to give a child true stability and emotional and physical security, to provide some domestic unit other than the biological family. Parents whose temperaments, tastes, and values are so fundamentally uncongenial that they really dislike each other, and whose home is filled with constant tension and discord, may do their children more serious and lasting harm by trying to endure the situation indefinitely than by frankly facing their incompatability and separating, rearranging their lives on a happier, healthier basis. They may sensibly and profitably and honestly separate "for the sake of the children."

Divorce is proof of a failure to love, and is almost invariably an even more unpleasant and expensive procedure than major surgery, yet there are occasions when it is necessary, even desirable. When? Whenever a marital relationship is difficult? No, because *all* intimate relationships that last any period of time involve difficulties, disagreements, and tensions, and spiritual growth is achieved when one lives through and learns from them. Many difficulties can and should be endured and surmounted, but some neither can nor should be. The famous "prayer for serenity" said by members of Alcoholics Anonymous is very much to the point here: "May God grant me the patience to endure what cannot be changed, the courage to change what should be changed, and the wisdom to know the difference."

Some people give up too easily. They have unrealistic expectations and make unfair demands. I remember a newspaper article about a woman who sued for divorce because her husband criticized her horseback riding form, and I remember a man who divorced his wife because she did not like it when he slid down the bannisters. But it is a sound old moral principle that the abuse of a thing does not justify the outlawing of its legitimate use. The existence of alcoholism does not mean alcohol should be against the law, said thirsty American churchmen before, during, and after Prohibition. Strong medicine may be very helpful when there is serious illness, even though it is a dangerous drug when taken too freely; divorce is strong medicine.

Why is the divorce rate rising in our era? Are people less adaptable and more selfish than in the past? There is no way of measuring how many marriages in the past were unhappy and whether, if legal and economic alternatives to marriage had then existed, many people would have taken advantage of them. Society as a whole is increasingly insecure today, for many complex reasons, and widespread divorce is a symptom of our unsolved social problems even more, I think, than it is a cause of them. Forbidding divorce would not make modern family life more stable and peaceful, any more than outlawing red spots would abolish measles. If and when we ever succeed in solving our major social problems, divorce may become as rare as scurvy after Vitamin C was discovered.

Though Bertrand Russell agreed with the Church about the desirability of permanent marriage where children are involved, he was much more merciful than the Church about punishing people who fail to achieve this goal. The Church gives them life sentences at solitary confinement with no hope of parole unless their fellow-failures die, a strictness more apt to make someone wish his "ex" were dead than to inspire increased charity. Russell insisted that the marital union must be *freely* chosen, not imposed by law. "It is not less binding because it is free," he said. "When the marital bond was a rigid framework, not easy and sometimes impossible to break, the conjugal partners within it might flaunt their revolts and persecute each other in private . . . (but) the day of hypocritical evasions is over."

In other words, parents should stay together because they want to, not because they have to. Is this type of thinking as unchristian as both Russell and his enemies would have us believe? Pharisaical religion demands strict conformity to rules regarding outward behavior, but Christ wants interior and voluntary goodwill. He tells us God listens to the secrets of our hearts, and judges us accordingly.

The family is, inevitably, strongest and most secure when it is economically profitable for people to live together. For centuries it was not only profitable but essential. It was impossible for women to support themselves unaided and to take care of their babies when the physical conditions of life were primitive and dangerous. Both men and women desired and needed many children; the more children there were, the more extra hands were available to help with the endless chores, and when the parents grew too tired and feeble to continue doing active physical work, as they did quite soon under harsh living conditions, their grown-up children became "their staff in old age," as stated in the Elizabethan *Book of Matrimony*. One needed to produce a lot of children to guarantee that a few would live long enough to perform this function.

Karl Marx was so aware of the family's financial *raisons d'etre* that he decided it was an economic institution invented by the bourgeoisie to protect property rights—though, inconsistently, he deeply loved his own family and one reason he hated capitalism so bitterly was that he could not bear to see his wife and children suffering from the effects of poverty. The institution, however, predates capitalism and is more basic than any economic system.

To be sure, one of the family's traditional functions has been to protect property, but not necessarily from a selfish motive: passing property along intact to one's children helped to grant them some security and hence a chance for happiness (as the wags say, "Money can't buy happiness but it helps.") Inheritance laws also helped to keep society as a whole more prosperous and stable. (Another example of how complicated it can be trying to tell right from wrong in human relationships is primogeniture: at first thought it seems unjust to leave all one's property to one's eldest son instead of dividing it equally, but it keeps land from being chopped into such small fragments that it becomes worthless. Countries, like India, where it is not practiced, succumb to increased poverty with each new generation. In Norway when primogeniture was not the royal family's custom there used to be a disastrous civil war in every generation; whenever a king died his sons fought over his divided domain until one of them had joined the king and the other had put the country back together again.)

It is desirable to have peace and to have enough to eat. When families are unable to preserve peace or provide food they collapse. The young may think it crass of their parents to be concerned about material things, and indeed it is not only crass but folly to be overconcerned, but what is today's revolution in the ghettos about if not at least in part man's universal need and right to have jobs, food, clothing, and shelter—in short, some degree of economic security?

In pioneer cultures, in eras of scarcity, in rural communities, in the premachine age, the family was an economic asset that provided some safety and even serenity; the family was everyone's security blanket. But living conditions have changed so enormously in the past century that this is no longer true, at least in the developed nations. The kind of work most needed today is not unskilled manual labor, and there is no longer enough for all those extra little hands to do —in fact, nowadays all poor parents notice in their children is all those extra mouths to feed. Far from being an economic advantage in a world of rising prices and housing shortages, a large family has become an economic liability, a luxury only the rich can afford.

Does this mean we should start sterilizing everybody and abolishing families? Of course not. We must change them greatly, however, and must start to consider quality more important than quantity.

This is basically a good change, an opportunity for hitherto undreamed-of progress, a giant step in humanity's advance, on the moral as well as economic level. We may no longer produce as many children as our ancestors did, but a larger number now survive and grow up healthy and well educated enough to make constructive and creative contributions to society. We can spend much more time with our children than parents used to be able to do, and therefore, in theory at least, can give them more helpful, more loving, and more intelligent guidance. The purpose of being born is not just to eat a few meals and then perish, but to have the opportunity to be born again and to grow in wisdom and grace, both giving and receiving gifts of spiritual value.

The Biblical admonition to "go forth and multiply" has more than been fulfilled since it was first commanded (to a world with a total population of eight people, according to Genesis). New York City alone now contains more people than lived in the entire continent of North America in 1816. We find it increasingly difficult to produce enough food to provide for a population that is doubling every few generations, and overcrowding is causing so many other problems (pollution, increased crime and delinquency, bad housing, traffic strangulation, and the like) that the entire quality of life is threatened. If we will recognize these new facts and respond to them appropriately, for the first time in history life, liberty, and the pursuit of happiness may be attainable for the majority of human beings.

If, instead, we continue to be guided by attitudes that grew out of *past* conditions, the generation gap will widen. If our children become confused and look to their contemporaries instead of to us for "communication" and value-formation we will have only ourselves to blame. If they "go to pot" (or worse) because self-destruction is a logical response to the frustrations of living in a self-destructive society, it will be because we are not reacting quickly or thoroughly enough to our changed circumstances. Too many people are still obsessed with acquiring material possessions in an era characterized by abundance rather than scarcity; they devote all their energies to earning a living in an era when creative leisure is possible; produce more children than they can cope with satisfactorily in an era when birth limitation is both possible and desirable; do not keep up with newly available educational and cultural opportunities, and do not expand their minds and hearts in an era that has been transformed by the expansion of technology.

Today *all* ideas and ideals are being boldly questioned, even very fundamental ones. This is inevitable, as universal education, rapid transportation, and worldwide communication make us increasingly aware of many differing codes. This does not mean all sacred ideas will be discarded. Gamaliel said to the Pharisees shocked by Christ's seeming blasphemy: "If this is of God it will stand." We need to cultivate Gamaliel's confidence in God's providence and really believe that He is omniscient, omnipotent and eternal Truth.

Anything that is permanently true will be true permanently, a tautology so obvious no one should require the reassurance that comes from uttering it. Anything of truly permanent value will survive temporary social upheavals and intellectual competition, though it may have to endure severe testing before its true value is conclusively proved.

As Baron von Hugel once wrote, people are always thinking that the barnacles that collect on a ship's hull are part of the hull, but it is necessary to keep scraping them off, and each new generation of Catholics must apply itself to that task if the bark of Peter is to stay afloat and seaworthy. Clumsy overeager youngsters may scratch the paint and even damage the hull sometimes by vigorous scrubbing, but a basically well-built ship can be repainted and repaired and will continue to carry people safely.

One of the profound messages of this era, characterized by such rapid and sweeping change, seems to be that "we have here no lasting city." As St. Teresa said, "All things change. God alone changeth not." He is the only ultimate truth, the only thing (precisely because he is not a "thing") that is in all respects permanent and unalterable. Social institutions are structures and arrangements established in response to human needs and conditions, and as those keep varying so do the institutions. We long for something permanent to depend on, and so we should; we are made for God and our hearts are restless until they rest in Him. We seek permanence instinctively. But when we look for it in anything other than God we are idolaters, looking in the wrong place.

Is the modern family really worse off than previous families? We tend to see things that are near us as exaggeratedly large, and things that are far away look smaller and less important, so we are more aware of today's woes and worries than of the problems that afflicted family life in the past. When we talk about the family's instability, we think of the current divorce rate (the U.S. rate is the highest in the world) or the increasing fashionableness of extra-marital sex or the generation gap. Instead, why not think of the steadily decreasing infant mortality rate? or the unprecedentedly low maternal death rate? or the incredible increase in fathers' life expectancy? (In ancient Rome the average man lived only 22 years; at the time of the American Revolution things were much better—he did not die until age 36. Today he stays around until 75.)

Families were disrupted in the past just as tragically and often as today, but by different causes. A high percentage of young mothers died in childbirth. Half the children died before reaching adulthood (as they still do in low-income countries). Middle-aged mothers were feeble and dependent. Most children had to do heavy, health- and mind-destroying manual labor. Unemployment was widespread. Luxuries and even necessities were scarce. Law and order was so unstable that men had to carry guns whenever they went outdoors. Margaret Mead has pointed out that the anxiety so common in modern civilization is a comfortable state of mind compared to that of people living in primitive societies: terror.

Family life in some periods of the past had unpleasant characteristics: dictatorial fathers, brow-beaten mothers, appallingly severe punishment of the young (whippings, ear-boxing, or imprisonment in dark closets), and cruelty to children with special problems (physical or mental defects or emotional difficulties). Survival of the fittest prevailed with ruthless efficiency. If our ethical ideal is that of ancient Sparta then we should consider today's family with its sentimental concern to protect and to help the mentally retarded and physically handicapped child as well as the "superior" child, retrogressive and even unnatural. But if our ideal is merciful love as described by Christ who said "whatever you do for the least of my brothers you do for Me," then we should admire the modern American family more than any of its predecessors.

Are youngsters who experiment with drugs much more depraved than the traditional drunken fathers who neglected their children and beat their wives regularly? Are youngsters who experiment with sex a more serious threat to family life than the pathetic women who have become so bitter and exhausted trying to raise ten children in harrowing poverty that they risk illegal abortions or have physical or mental breakdowns?

People who think the pill is ruining morality and causing couples to forget the connection between sex and parenthood should stop to realize that families have always endeavored to control their size, and the means they used were much less fastidious than swallowing a pill: witches' potions, abortions, child abandonment, exposure, and infanticide. The Church officially calls the pill "unnatural," but *all* medicines and surgical operations and mechanical devices are attempts to interfere with natural conditions. Why object to a diaphragm that keeps sperm out of a womb, but not to an electric fence that keeps cows out of a pasture? The Church objects to sterilization, but for centuries permitted castration of boys in order to produce good soprano church choirs, and St. Thomas Aquinas approved of punishing criminals by castration. The Church objects to reducing the population by using an interuterine device, but with much less unambiguous indignation to reducing it by using bullets. The Church condemns abortion, but the highest abortion rates in the world are in Catholic South America.

Men have always enjoyed sexual freedom via prostitutes. The Church, though appalled at the thought of divorce becoming legal in Italy, has realistically accepted the legality of prostitution for a long time. Is it really more immoral for a man to find his physical recreation with a girl of whom he is genuinely fond and who is fond of him, than with a girl who degrades her body by treating it as a commercial commodity? Will it not be moral progress if an entire class of women no longer has to endure permanent humiliation and segregation in order to protect the chastity of other women? May not the pill, or an even more efficient future invention, mean that people may become less selfish, less exploitative of others, as well as that only people who really want children will have them, and therefore all children will come into families ready to give them far more emotional security and stability than was assured them in the past when they were spawned by chance?

There is pain, often excruciating pain, in modern family life. Children suffer acutely from separation and divorce and insecurity; so do deserted husbands and wives and neglected old people, perhaps more keenly and more often than in the past, but perhaps merely more openly and noticeably. I remember an old lady who, on her deathbed, in delirium, revealed anguish she had kept secret for over fifty years. She realized on her wedding day that she had married the wrong boy. She lived more than half a century with a man she did not love, never revealing it. Some would say this was heroic virtue; others might say it was lifelong hypocrisy. Even if we consider her heroic, is it necessary or right to sacrifice one's personal happiness to this extent? It was necessary for her; when she was young there was no such thing as legal divorce and women could not earn a living, so she was stuck. Today she would probably extricate herself and try again; might she not end up a happier, more creative, and more loving person? Undoubtedly her groom would have suffered if she had left him, but perhaps he too would have recovered from the shock and even have found someone else to share his life, someone who would have loved him as she did not. In later life he was a very grouchy man, whose children feared and despised him; maybe his heroic wife's inability to love him helped to make him grouchy.

Christians emphasize that love is a matter of the will: we can concentrate on seeking out a person's good qualities and on doing loving things for the person and grow in love of him or her as a result of our attitude. St. John of the Cross said, "Where you find no love, put love and you will find love." Psychologists confirm that we are more apt to love a person we do things for than a person who does things for us. But are not some people truly uncongenial, not because one is good and the other bad but just because they are enormously different, so that even with genuine mutual goodwill they cannot make each other happy, although they do not realize this until too late? And if parents are basically unhappy, is it possible for their children to be happy? Children need to be surrounded by happiness as much as plants need sunshine.

What God has joined together no man should tear asunder. This is true, and always will be. But more often than we like to acknowledge, it may not be God (Love) that brings people to the altar or keeps them under one roof. Lust, neurotic anxiety, economic opportunism, social ambition, and smug conventionality are among the wolves that are sometimes disguised in a sheepish bride's or groom's clothing.

As new psychological insights become deeper and more widespread, so that people become more understanding and tolerant and hence more patient with each other's (and their own) real needs and limitations, there should be a greater chance than ever before to produce happy and good families. Parents will learn more about *how* to teach as well as *what* to teach their children.

We must learn to ask ourselves, "Is this a loving thing to do?" rather than "Is this a conventional . . . or popular . . . or traditional . . . or safe . . . or profitable . . . thing to do?" We must learn to ask ourselves this question with a degree of candor exceeding the superficial examinations of conscience so many of us made in the past with the aid of standardized, prefabricated lists of sins, rattling off *mea culpas* by rote, which we often did sincerely but with an abysmal lack of real psychological insight into our motives and feelings so that we lied to ourselves without knowing it.

We will be in for some surprises, and will find that some of the things we used to do that we thought were loving were not, and some things we thought were not loving were.

Love is meant to include but also to extend beyond the family. Which is more important: love of parents? of neighbor? of enemies? of children? of self? of God? Christ equates them all.

Will the family survive this century? That question is similar to another many people are asking today: Will the Church survive? To both questions my answer is yes; unless we blow up the entire world with nuclear weapons, or choke ourselves to death with pollution, we will not blow up or strangle the family or the Church.

If only one healthy man and woman are left, the family will survive (though incest taboos will have to be abolished for a few generations) because it is a biological, psychological, social, and cultural necessity. Men and women have an instinctive desire to establish intimate and lasting relationships with each other, and part of that desire inevitably and naturally expresses itself in sexuality, which produces children, and children need to be taken care of through the very type of intimate, long-range human relationships that their parents desire instinctively. It is a lovely, unvicious circle. Human babies, unlike newborn giraffes, cannot toddle around on their own a few hours after they are born; they need prolonged protection and care, and their helplessness inspires it. The process of helping someone is maturing and civilizing. It creates and increases tenderness and consideration, a reciprocal flow of generosity and gratitude and mutual affection. That is the essence of the family: people living together and helping each other because they need and want each other.

The Church will survive for similar reasons: people have a basic need or desire to establish an intimate and lasting relationship with their creator, and part of that relationship is expressed in prayer and involves seeking comfort and inspiration by developing forms of worship that can be shared with other people.

In short, both institutions will survive as long as humans do because both meet basic human aspirations. But will either institution survive in the precise form they have today? My answer is no, because people who live in space-time are always and inevitably changing, and always and inevitably influencing each other so that society and its institutions also change, and in the twentieth century this process has been speeded up to a degree that makes many of us dizzy. We meet more new people and new influences in one month than most people did in an entire lifetime a few centuries ago, so it is no wonder that we ourselves are more changeable than our ancestors were. There are so many more factors to change us. Durable relationships are harder to maintain because people who at one stage in their lives are a help and solace to each other may develop along different lines and end up in conflict. Instead of viewing this with alarm, as a sign of increasing instability, we can try thinking of it as evidence of increasing flexibility; instead of regarding it as a problem to be regretted we can think of it as a challenge to develop more facets of our character and an opportunity to find more outlets for our talents and virtues than the limited environments of the past could offer anyone.

In what new forms will the family and the Church survive? Which of their present characteristics will last? We do not know. Time carries us forward, never backward; we always have to travel without being able to see where we are going. This is hard, and sometimes scary. Timid pessimists are inclined, like the panicky members of Columbus's crew, to fear that they are heading toward the end of the world, to destruction. We need to acquire the genuine humility that enables one to live peacefully with the understanding that one's knowledge is very limited. We must develop the genuine faith that accepts uncertainty without anxiety, trusting not in our own finite wisdom and strength but in God's infinite power. It is not necessary for us to know what the future holds; it is enough for our welfare that God knows.

The family, as the most universal and basic of all human institutions, is bound to be intimately affected by all the changes that affect its members. The economic, social, political, military and racial conflicts, tensions, pressures, and insecurities that have been caused by the unprecedented acceleration of changes in the modern world, produce loud and discordant echoes in our homes, upsetting peaceful family life. The Lord of the universe, however, he whom even the winds and the rains and the waves of the sea obey, quiets storms in His own time. This storm too shall pass.

Change, growth, and readjustment are not easy or comfortable processes, as any teething baby or gangling adolescent or woman in labor knows. Not comfortable, but very, very rewarding. Not easy, but very, very exciting. When one learns to replace fear of the unknown with trust in the loving God who is leading us into the unknown, one is free to respond to new challenges with eagerness instead of reluctance. Freedom is one of humanity's greatest glories, worth the risks, problems and even pains it entails. Christians are meant to consider themselves children of freedom rather than slaves to law, so why should they fear that the great longing for greater freedom that is causing upheavals all over the world should be a threat to the Christian family or the Christian Church? Specific changes may startle, puzzle, inconvenience, or annoy us; some we will dislike while we enjoy others, some we will personally welcome and some we will personally reject—the prerogative of our own personal freedom. Change in itself we must not reject; it is a fundamental condition of our being.

Institutions that are too rigid or limited to change disappear and are replaced in the course of time, but those which exist because they answer fundamental human needs adapt. Insofar as any specific church or family is too unimaginative or timid or lazy to change, in response to the explosions of knowledge and inventions and population that have altered almost every aspect of human life in the past fifty years, it will be unable to survive (and will not deserve to) because it will thereby demonstrate that it cannot meet new conditions and is no longer useful. Therefore, when we see changes taking place in both the family and the Church, we should rejoice, instead of feeling disturbed. These changes are proof that these institutions are truly human, relevant and valuable, resilient and strong, and capable of making the transitions required by a transitional age.

It is by being flexible, responsive, and creative—in short, by changing—that the family will endure. The ability to change is a sign of vigorous life, not of death.

FAMILY LIFE: THE
AGONY AND THE ECSTASY 3

Paul Marx and Jack Quesnell

Marriage seems more popular than ever. The family, however, while carrying the burden of multiple problems, is changing swiftly. Enormous published literature on marriage and family life evidences a deepening interest in and concern about the family in a time of unique and accelerating change. Even if there is a reciprocal relation between person and community as well as between family and society, the family *is* the barometer of the nation, in fact, of the whole family of mankind. Anyone, therefore, seriously interested in human welfare and the future of man in a changing culture must concern himself with the inner dynamics of family life, especially as it is *the* channel of culture and *the* agency of socialization.

THE FAMILY TODAY— WHAT HAS HAPPENED?

Adults who think that the frenetic modern world will once again settle down; that issues will again be black or white; that the generational "grand canyon" will again become the traditional "gap" are naive. Human knowledge is now doubled every seven years. Information explodes. The United States government alone annually invests more than seventeen billion dollars in that great engine of change: basic research. Consider only the last decade's developments in space, computer science, cybernetics, molecular biology, and the medical sciences, to see how swiftly new knowledge is harnessed in technology; how soon the whole culture is altered; and how swiftly the impact on human and family living is felt.

Perhaps we can understand the problems of the family better if we think of this as an age of multiple revolutions. Consider, for example, the Erotic or Sexual Revolution. According to the best research, this revolution is largely a profound change of attitudes. Rooted in changing values, attitudes propel behavioral change. Young people follow with interest and dismay the debates over celibacy, premarital sex, birth control, and abortion. For some, their anguish is intensified by the unprecedented, world-wide unfavorable reaction and the crisis of authority in the Church precipitated by *Humanae Vitae*. The confused young are constantly reminded of the overpopulation problem. They are the targets of the subtle seeking after abortion-on-demand as a human right in almost every state. The justification and merits of premarital intercourse are debated on every campus in terms of to bed or not to bed, without a hint that not on bed alone doth man live.

The more than 750,000 illegitimate pregnancies annually in our country should tell us something. This, of course, would include the more than 300,000 babies born out of wedlock in 1968. Another indication: the past year's one-and-a-half million new cases of gonorrhea. Nor have the young been untouched by the many articles pleading for a loosening of the divorce laws of the Church. It has been said *Playboy* is read by boys so young that they think all girls have staples at the navel. Meanwhile, frantic efforts to launch sex-education programs in schools are often opposed by parents who still think of sex in terms of plumbing. As Frank Sheed commented, few adults have *thought* much about human sexuality. They have mostly emoted and played and drooled over sex, the pitfalls of which they now wish to spare their children. Human sexuality may be "the last bastion of ignorance" and involve "the greatest number of myths and superstitions," as Dr. Leon Salsman has pointed out, but it will take decades before a large portion of Americans see human sexuality as more than genitality, that is, understand it as pervading and illuminating an integrated personality with quite serious implications for a healthy spirituality. Like-the iceberg in the water, the psychological and spiritual dimensions of sexuality lie deep in one's personhood.

Again, all too few realize the extent of the philosophical revolution, the advance of Existentialism, the modern interest in Situation or Contextual Ethics, and the New Morality which someone all too simply called the "old lust." This revolution in thought, this posing of new questions or this uncovering of new facets of old problems, alone goes far in explaining why parents frequently do not understand even the questions of their adolescents. From social psychology we learn that human beings tend to respond not to reality but to a mental picture of reality built up over the years. In a time of exploding information and instant sight-and-sound communication, parents can be almost totally out of touch with the existential world. In a sense, never have they had more to learn from the young.

Also, medical breakthroughs expressed, for example, in organ transplants, new drugs, differing definitions of death, as well as the pill-culture face the Christian with many new situations; in the foreseeable future theologians will be far behind in formulating viable moral norms. No wonder moral theology is in a shambles, the science of ethics is in ferment, and the Canon Law just now being revamped will be outdated even before it is published. Small wonder, too, that there should be faith crises on every level, especially in the young who grow up with little adult consensus and then are systematically taught to doubt, to dissent, to question, and to demonstrate—for *what* is not always clear. Never have there been so many angry rebels without a program. The complicated issues of peace and war, authority and freedom, clerical and religious defections, disagreement in the Church on every level of authority, the precarious state of Catholic and public education, the choking ecumenism, the racial minority and student revolutions—all of these remind one of the line in the play, *Green Pastures,* concerning the deluge: "All dat was nailed down is comin' loose." Asked his opinion of liturgical changes, an old man responded, "Yes, they've changed everything but the collection." Or as a cynic said of the Dutch Mass, "Everything is changed but the bread and wine."

In the past the prevailing culture was often an intelligible extension of an organic and developing tradition. Not so, today. In terms of cultural change a generation is perhaps five years. And hence, the lengthening generational gap, now better described as a grand canyon; across this parents find it painful, if not impossible, to communicate with their offspring. Paul VI put it well when he spoke of the cause of unique tension everywhere in terms of "the discovery of ever-increasing possibilities, of unforeseeable conquests through scientific exploration, and the technical domination of nature"; he implied also the domination of human beings. To this he added "the observation of the conditions of need in which, under so many aspects, the greater part of mankind lives."

Still other changes affect us. In a few decades the family has known the effects of a rapid shift from a rural, small-town way of life to an urban, industrialized society. Almost seventy-five percent of Americans already live in cities, on less than two percent of the land; by 1980 it is estimated that eighty-five percent of Americans will reside in some two hundred metropolitan complexes. In a simpler age Dad was home for three meals a day; early in life the family had a little task for each youngster; children constituted an economic asset, security for old age; and the family did many things together. Today it often costs more to keep the young entertained than was spent on Dad's education. In today's nuclear family of parents and children living in suburbia or the city, father leaves home early in the morning; the children are in the hands of the harassed wife who, after conversation with three- and four-footers all day, craves the companionship and intellectual challenge of her husband. He, tired of having been nice to everybody all day, would rather sit in a soft chair, read the evening paper or watch TV, and drink his cocktail.

Although females today experience the menarche earlier and menopause later, there is increasing control over birth and death, giving women manifold options as to their life-work. The result? Rapid family change and role confusion, making the familial unit even more vulnerable to many powerful pressures our forefathers on the farm or in the village never knew. Today about half the American girls are married at twenty and have a median number of about three children as they reach the median age of completed family size at twenty-six or twenty-seven; then, not surprisingly, when the last child is in school, and sometimes before that, they look elsewhere for the job or career satisfactions of which their forebears did not dream.

Currently only one out of every eighteen Americans live on the farm. Given the increasing need of protracted education and the consequent need for delaying marriage while physically and psychologically ready, though not so economically and educationally, it is easy to see why young people cannot follow all the ways and rules of their parents' youth.

Another factor profoundly affecting the family is the amazing development of instant mass communication making the world a kind of global village. For the first time in history men have *seen* the earth from the reaches of outer space. Even before the child spends his first day in kindergarten he has been stimulated by three to four thousand hours of TV; by the time he has graduated from high school, he has spent more than eleven thousand hours before what the psychiatrist Karl Stern called "that electronic box pumping pleasure into people." Today's college sophomores do not remember a time when there was no TV. Some 400-million people at one and the same time saw Churchill buried. Hardly was the assassinated President Kennedy in the hospital when most of the world was participating in the emotion-packed drama via television.

In the words of Marshall McLuhan, "The family circle has widened. The whirlpool of information fathered by electric media . . .

far surpasses any possible influence Mom and Dad can now bring to bear. Character is no longer shaped by only two earnest, fumbling experts. Now all the world's a sage." Stimulated from all sides by diverse ideologies and conflicting values, the young see that so many ways of thinking and rules of even the recent past no longer fit new realities; they tend to distrust anyone over thirty, while their parents may trust no one under fifty, hence, the generational grand canyon. As Margaret Mead has said, the young are more at home in the culture, understand it better, having grown up with it, while their parents are like "immigrants" groping their way as if in the dark, often befuddled and bewildered, often distrusted by the Now Generation. All too often the restive young escape from an unhappy home bristling with tension, or from a world seething with possibilities of more wars, into what they consider will be the romantic paradise of marriage. They easily forget what the Pennsylvania Dutch so well say, "Kissin' don't last; cookin' do." Wider yawns the gap that separates the young, born and raised in affluence or even luxury, from their parents who have personally experienced the hardships of a depression and the rigors of a world war. The parents wonder where they have failed. For this reason alone we need to take a good hard look at family life education at every level and instigate postmarital workshops on family living in a new cultural context.

Perhaps the best way to begin is to take a good hard look at the way young people are thinking about love, sexuality, and marriage. Venerated ideas of yesteryear like "the bonds of marriage," "the institution of marriage," or the "vocation of marriage" no longer impress a growing number of the young. Nor do they stand at attention when someone speaks of the "sacramentality of marriage" or marriage as "lifelong commitment"—notions they can hardly understand, given the ever more common "Why marry?" attitude. Where love is freely given, why speak of vows? Given the freedom of choice to love each other, why speak of contract? Young people who hold these views or ask these questions are like the Barnard coed last year who, after having been upbraided for living with a man not her husband, calmly replied to the question whether she would marry this individual by stating, "David and I do not believe in marriage."

Such young people of the Now Generation do not easily see the consequences that result from marriage becoming a purely consensual affair between two individuals. They are not aware that their "love freely given" is most likely neither free nor love. This is not an age that appreciates the radically social character of human nature and indeed of marriage itself. True, the decision to marry or to engage in a marriage relationship is a most personal one, but it inherently involves many others. Because of the eminently social consequences stemming from this most personal decision and thus involving the community and inherently a public commitment along with a private promise or vow, all of human experience and anthropological data point to the need of some kind of public witness before two people live together "in love" as committed partners. Dietrich Bonhöffer, the famed Lutheran martyr-theologian, admonished the young in his *A Wedding Lesson from a Prison Cell:* "Your love is your own private possession, but marriage is more than something personal—it is a status, an office."

When the Communists came into power in Russia in 1917, they attempted to abolish the family as the bourgeois haven of the worst turpitudes of the capitalist past; they abolished the marriage ceremony, forbade the manufacture of wedding rings, and allowed "marriage" with a mere notification at an agency to which a postcard could then be sent if divorce was desired later. By 1935, the Communists made an about-face: They found out that love is not in the glands, that free love is neither free nor love, and that any careless tampering with human sexuality strikes at the very heart and health of person and society.

Neither the individual person nor society, then, is served by misconceiving the true nature of human sexuality, human love, and marriage. As every experienced counselor knows, quasi-marital pairings or casual sexual relationships established in defiance of parents, religion, or society are actually more miserable than not; such liaisons are characteristically compulsive, driven, shallow, often entered into in order to ward off depression, emotional isolation, or the painful inadequacies of immaturity. Such attempts at realizing sexual freedom only create more delusion and more psychological enslavement.

In a sex-soaked culture which so easily deceives so many, young people need to think long and hard on the true nature of psychological freedom, human love, and sexuality, as well as of marriage as total commitment if they want their marriage to be what Vatican II said every marriage should be: "An intimate partnership of life and love together." They need to distinguish carefully between physical sex and genuine human love. As Jacques Maritain once said, "The first truth about marriage is that love is not sex." On the other hand, they must see their human sexuality as pervading their whole personality—indeed their very spirituality—just as they need to face again and again the truth in Gerald Vann's statement, "You don't make love; love makes you."

"I-love-you-so-why-not-live-together?" easily descends to "I-am-tired-of-you-and-so-will-leave-you." Love "freely given" is also "freely withheld." A person freely used in the name of love is also freely abandoned. How transitory are words of love that stem only from physical desire! What trust in the other's integrity is generated by the so-called love-acts in a motel room made available through a lie told the desk clerk? Sin is not a popular notion today. But the conduct that it describes still exists. Ralph Waldo Emerson's words still make their point, "Men are not so much punished *for* their sins as *by* their sins."

The wrecked lives and homes occasioned by an increasing divorce rate, if not St. Francis de Sales' remark that "marriage is the most difficult of all vocations," should at least slow down those who would rush in where so many convinced of their love have failed or are failing. Surely it is wise to distrust emotion, at least somewhat, and to think seriously, to shore up one's character by faithful prayer and a good confession (if Catholic) or by a spiritual conference with one's pastor (if not Catholic); to seek some specific instructions from a clergyman, coupled with suitable reading and discussion; and to wed in a religious ceremony attended by family and friends who at the very least can give psychological support then and later. Before marriage a boy and girl so easily say, "Our marriage or living together is our business." But let that marriage break, and it will then become everyone's business.

Not even a married couple is an island, as all newlyweds soon learn. Strange indeed is a love which stems from a mentality that says: "I will love you until I no longer like you, or until someone else comes along who attracts me more." Does not this happen every day? Were not those equally serious who in addition proclaimed in the past their "love" publicly and who vowed before God's altar that they would love each other forever? It may seem strange to say "I love you for three years," or "I love you until . . . ," but have not many "loves" in the past amounted to little more than that even if solemnly rendered before God and man? And will the so-called noninstitutional of ceremoniless marriage amounting to hardly more than quasi-marital pairing do better?

The extended comments of the late Protestant theologian Karl Barth are entirely to the point:

> Vocation to marriage is vocation to this life-partnership. To this extent marriage is more than love. It must spring from love if it is to take shape as a genuine life-partnership. It must always be fed and sustained by love if it is to have firm subsistence as such. . . . The essence of marriage is more comprehensive than what we must understand by the term love in the sense of the special love of husband and wife. It consists essentially in the life-partnership established and subsisting between these two. As such it is the consummation of what is sought and striven for in genuine love. Marriage as a life-partnership is the touchstone whether or not the seeking and striving was and is that of genuine love. Marriage as a life-partnership is therefore the proof of love. In marriage as a life-partnership it is a matter of repeating in all seriousness the *YES* of love. But "in all seriousness" means in a life which is the whole life of man, in toil and care, in joy and pain, in sickness and health, in youth and age, in wrestling with the many questions, small and great, inner and outer, individual and social, which lovers united in a common life can and may as little evade as other men, but all these things in the fellowship of their life, in some way or other together, in the special orientation of the one or the other, in the evenness of step between the two selected and willed for this purpose. "In all seriousness" means experiencing all this in the succession of unforeseeably many days of twenty-four hours and unforeseeably many years of fifty-two

weeks, with the intimacy of an every day and every night companionship which discloses everything on both sides, in which each very soon gets to know the other with terrifying exactitude, and in which the greatest thing can become astonishingly small and the smallest astonishingly great. "In all seriousness" means to have become a collective, a *WE,* a pair, and to live as such, not merely outwardly, but inwardly as the only possible basis of the outward, and not merely in the life of mutual relations, but in the thinking, willing, and feeling of both participants upon which these relations must rest if they are to be tenable. This seriousness of love is what we mean by marriage as a life-partnership. And when love stands the test of this seriousness, it means that marriage is a partnership which is fulfilled not merely according to the claims of duty, but gladly, joyfully, and willingly, in repetition of the *YES* of love.*

Surely no one could understand adequately the problems of marriage and parenting today who would not make allowance for a resurgent feminism. The very names of Friedan-Callahan-Daly-Reuther-Ellmann send shivers down some male backs and remind us of the changing role of women. To the changing female expectations, men must adjust. Ask girls in a marriage preparation course whether they think much beyond future husband, a small flock of children, their hoped-for family, and they will admit they hardly consider much else so far as their future life is concerned. And yet, thirty-six percent of the American work force is female; one of seven wives ends up supporting her children singly; more than fifty-eight percent of working women are married; between the ages of nineteen and sixty-five the average American female works some twenty-six years outside the home. On the average, one-half of married life is lived with one's spouse (if the marriage has lasted) as the "empty-nest" phenomenon comes earlier than ever. Thus, while going through the child bearing-rearing-launching years, mother does well to keep sharpened, insofar as possible, any other acquired vocational skills. Perhaps Catholic girls more than others still suffer from an excessive

* Karl Barth, *On Marriage,* a Facet Book (Philadelphia: Fortress Press, 1968).

"motherhood syndrome." In a society where most will have a short-ened, bunched pregnancy period of less than a decade and where they will actually have two careers, marriage-family and job-outside-the-home, the educational experience of girls has to be considerably altered. Obviously, here, too, there is cultural lag.

This brings us to the painful birth-control dilemma and the papal interdiction of contraception. The control of death and no commensurate control of birth has brought on a rapid expansion of population. Within thirty years sixty percent of the world's population will be less than twenty-one years of age. Never in the history of mankind have human females been so fertile for so long. In the *Wealth of Nations* (1776) Adam Smith wrote, "It is not uncommon . . . in the Highlands of Scotland for a mother who has borne twenty children not to have two alive." He goes on to say that in many places in England half the children died before they were four, and almost everywhere half the children only lived to the age of nine or ten. Until 100 years ago one-half of the children once born died before they were six. Even today one-half die in India before they reach the age of five. As late as 1918, the Spanish influenza killed 21 million across the world, including 548,452 in America.

Some eighty of one hundred American couples need 10–15–20 years of fertility control. Rhythm or periodic abstinence is no solution in the present context for very many. Given present fertility levels, a couple resorting only to rhythm as their means of birth control would spend a good half of their fertile life abstaining. There is no notable difference in family size between Catholics and Protestants. The fact is that Catholics *do* practice contraceptive birth control. According to the best studies, between fifty and sixty percent of Catholics in childbearing years have at one time, or are presently, practicing contraception. In an age of the large family and lengthy childbearing years, woman's central and primary role was bearing and rearing children. Today there is an historical reversal. Only a part of her life is taken up with rearing a family. Whereas formerly it was her social responsibility to spend most of her life in the home caring for children, today many say it is her social responsibility not to rear so many children.

Meanwhile, in almost every state there are strong pleas for abortion-on-demand as a means of birth control and as a way of promoting "female emancipation." Liberalized abortion laws and the new, simpler abortive techniques would for many take away the very motive for contraception. The incidence of venereal disease and homosexuality has risen alarmingly; so, too, illegitimacy as sexual activity has been divorced from procreation-education. The young often identify love as "feeling." The Playboy Philosophy is rampant: "Sex with love is better, but sex without love is fun too—so why not have both?"

The thrust of Situation Ethics and the New Morality represents no small threat. Harvard's Dr. Graham B. Blaine defines the New Morality "as simply a linking of total sexual experience with love rather than, as in the old morality, an equating of total sexual experience with marriage." Christians cannot accept this bed-sex concept of love and marriage. Many are the indications that the contraceptive mentality brings with it premarital intercourse, abortion, a train of other sexual abuses, and possibly even paves the way for acceptance of euthanasia. Even so, some have argued this would not necessarily forbid contraception to the loving couple wishing to be generous and responsible before God.

The condemnation of contraceptive birth control in *Humanae Vitae* was explicitly not given as infallible teaching. The question then arises, how does a noninfallible though authoritative and authentic teaching of the Magisterium oblige in conscience? In the religious instruction of the past this question was never faced. The best explanation of the best theologians—that noninfallible though official moral teaching of the Church cannot bind in each and every circumstance—does not wipe away the anxiety of many couples who have been taught the evil of artificial birth control and who have been raised to think nothing could change and all the Church's teaching is infallible. The confusion is compounded, although consolation is given to many, by the commentaries on the encyclical by a number of national hierarchies to the effect that couples in difficult circumstances may make a sincere decision of conscience in the matter to save all the values of marriage. For example, the French hierarchy said that contraception is always a disorder, but not necessarily always sinful. Even these statements of national hierarchies are confusing and actually contradictory. However, since the clarification of collegiality at the last Roman synod, notable theological authorities have pointed out that *Humanae Vitae* was not the fruit of collegial thinking and decision, and to that extent it is not seriously binding.

Undoubtedly, the Christian family, buffeted by so many conflicting values and so much bad example, will have to trudge a difficult and winding road ahead, pockmarked with doubt and discomforts. All the more so because Christians are becoming a dwindling number; it will be harder to hold to a certain, demanding way of life not welcome in the larger society. Nor is this all. With fewer priests and religious, less formal Catholic education, no adequate adult-education programs, and no professionally trained laity to teach religion, Christians will indeed be the People of God in the wilderness of heathenism and luxury, for which even Benjamin Franklin admitted there has never been found a remedy. In this connection we do well to heed Bishop Sheen's admonition:

> The fewer sacrifices a man is required to make, the more loath he is to make those few. His luxuries become necessities, children a burden and the ego is god. Whence will come our heroes of a nation, if we no longer have heroes at home? If a man will not put up with the trials of a home, will he put up with the trials of a national crisis?

THE CHALLENGE OF MODERN PARENTHOOD

The Christian parent may look askance at a world in which he is a kind of "immigrant" feeling his way. Nevertheless, his sincerity compels him to clarify his vocational role and reflect upon the changing family. The dynamic, adaptive family will survive until Gabriel blows his trumpets calling all of us to join in the eternal joys of the Father's family in heaven. What remains of the traditional authoritarian family will fade into irrelevancy.

The committed and informed parent realizes that the agencies of society have assumed many of the functions of the traditional family. But one essential function remains, a function no other agency can fulfill, a function for which all others are ancillary: the formation of a loving, mature, and flexible personality that can adjust to the increasing vicissitudes of the future. Hence the contemporary parent must carefully oversee the agencies of society and decide to which he will expose his children. Within a technological society he creates a culturally and spiritually rich home environment. He guards against the danger that a computerized society will bend, fold, or mutilate the dignity, integrity, and worth of family members.

Obviously the parent remains as the primary influence in the life of the child. His aim is still to help the young learn to love, work, and develop healthy social relationships. The basic goal of preparing youth to realize a developing fulfillment and to live as educated social beings is constant. The Christian parent strives to accomplish this by helping his children attain the basic life-tasks conceptualized by Erik Erickson: developing a sense of trust, autonomy, initiative, industry, and a sense of identity. Therefore mothers and fathers must relate to the youth in such a manner that he acquires a positive perception of himself and others. The discreet parent listens with the "third ear" and discovers the rich meaning contained in Nolte's poem, "Children Learn What They Live":

> If a child lives with criticism,
>   He learns to condemn.
> If a child lives with hostility,
>   He learns to fight.
> If a child lives with ridicule,
>   He learns to be shy.
> If a child lives with shame,
>   He learns to feel guilty.
> If a child lives with tolerance,
>   He learns to be patient.
> If a child lives with encouragement,
>   He learns confidence.
> If a child lives with praise,

> He learns to appreciate.
> If a child lives with fairness,
>   He learns justice.
> If a child lives with security,
>   He learns to have faith.
> If a child lives with approval,
>   He learns to like himself.
> If a child lives with acceptance and friendship,
>   He learns to find love in the world.*

Only from the responsive and responsible love of parents will the family become, as Vatican II observed, "a school of deeper humanity."

The alert parent realizes that spouses must give constant attention to the primacy of the marital relationship. In general, loving children have parents who love each other. In *The Art of Loving,* Erich Fromm explains that love is not taught, but is learned from the earliest experiences of life. And if not in the home, where? Jacques LeClerq said, "The first thing parents owe their children is to love each other properly." Within such a family the elders and their children after them will embrace their sexuality as a gift and opportunity from God, appreciating it as suffusing the whole personality. Mothers will enjoy being women; fathers will enjoy being men. From the spiritual dynamo of a joyful home both will become aware of their potential for love and service to God's whole family of mankind. In a time of spousal role-confusion, husbands and wives will be flexible and respond to each other's unique human needs generated by an evolving society.

In an impersonal and pluralistic society the need for a keen appreciation of guiding principles and Christian values which point to "life beyond" is self-evident. Surely, if the parents lack familiarity with issues like the "New Morality" and have little awareness of theology's growing edge, their children may become tragic victims of the "revolutions" previously described.

In a world of burgeoning theological problems, and the conse-

* Reprinted by permission of the John Philip Co., 91 Lost Lake Lane, Campbell, Calif. 95008.

quent lack of clear-cut moral norms, it is enormously important for parents to understand the nature, formation, and function of an informed and formed conscience. This they must delicately cultivate in their offspring. The young no longer follow moral prescriptions simply because "the Church says so." They increasingly ask, Why? and their Whys must be intelligently answered. From the informed and loving practice of the faith in the "domestic Church," as Vatican II called the home, trusted children will learn to make responsible personal decisions within the context of broad moral guidelines. Of course, parents teach primarily by what they *are*. Like love, relevant religion is more caught than taught. According to St. Gregory the Great, the formation and guidance of youth is "the art of arts and the science of sciences." A child needs the attentive ear of an informed parent as he sorts out and clarifies the conflicting values and opposing norms pumped into him by the communications media. The knowledgeable and affectionate parent "environs" his offspring with the proper values and principles and then motivates him to grasp *what is* and to pursue *what ought to be*. According to Leo XIII, we must see this world as it really exists and often look elsewhere for the solace of its troubles.

THE PARENT—MEMBER OF TOMORROW'S FAMILY

For the world of tomorrow the Christian family today will strive toward an egalitarian ideal that respects the unique capacities of each member. As the parent attempts to evaluate the child's behavior and clarify standards, he will recognize that what is acceptable at one developmental stage is not necessarily acceptable at another; what is attainable at adolescence is not possible in childhood. The educator of youth will recognize the creative individuality of each child and not clamp him into the "Iron Maiden" forged of parental dreams and false societal expectations. He will approach the vocation of parenthood as the artist who has confidence that the picture on the canvas will take shape, realizing there is no one pattern into which the child *must* fit. He will lead the child in discovering his potential.

This entails cultivating interpersonal relationships. Giving and receiving of affection, the growing realization of equality between husband and wife, joint decision-making increasingly involving the whole family, the developing personhood of each member—these characterize the healthy, emerging family. Meanwhile, family members will seek to fulfill their own potential and balance this effort with an equal desire to help other members fulfill their capacities. In the family where decisions result from consensus there is no room for a "paycheck" husband or dictator-head who assails family members with his self-centered opinions and aspirations.

To the extent that parents are the first and most vital teachers, a growing child requires various parental approaches. At one time the parent-teacher prods, directs, and leads. At other times, and especially during adolescence, the young react best to a teacher who is more of a counselor. He provides a relationship within which the teen-ager can give expression to his own ideas and goals, profit from his own sometimes even erratic experiences, and sort out his own feelings within the limits of reasonable freedom. These differing approaches of the parents are all made within an atmosphere of consistent and loving discipline.

The ideal home environment generates an increasing thirst for knowledge. The Jewish family gives expression to this by strewing the child's first book with raisins and almonds, symbolizing the sweetness of knowledge. After all, by the age of four, a child forms half the intelligence he will have at maturity. In fact, studies in child development suggest that intellectual acumen grows as much during the first four years of life as it will during the next thirteen. Research also indicates that by age six, a child attains two-thirds of the intelligence he will have at seventeen. Finally the potential for psychological, intellectual, and spiritual growth between four and seventeen is influenced significantly by life experiences prior to age four.

Accordingly the "tuned-in" parent will critically examine the significance of canyonistic gaps between generations. He will seek only to bridge the chasms, not to merge the various generations into a homogeneous mass. He will especially guard against the danger of comparing the cultural climate of his own youth with that of his youngsters. These are two different worlds. Here, too, comparisons are odious. Besides, was the past really that good and exemplary? Parents often conveniently forget how they, too, learned through a process of trial and error.

Studies of adolescent society indicate that teen-agers expect from their parents intelligent and loving guidance. Parental ineptitude, irrelevance, and an unwillingness to learn or dialogue indicates weakness or disinterest. Such parental inadequacies are resented and exploited by the young. In a transitional world of complex diversity the young have an added right to examine the ideals of their elders, and even improve on them. Painful as the thought may be to some, children have been known to make saints out of their long-suffering parents. St. Benedict asked religious superiors to consult the young, because God often reveals new insights to them. Only a meaningful dialogue between parents and offspring will forge the girders and anchor the moorings of the bridge across the generational gap. Tomorrow's sound family will welcome evolutionary change and technological advance, balanced by spiritual growth, total cultural development, and theological inquiry. The parents of such a family will have to take increasing responsibility for the moral and religious education and rearing of their children.

Will the family survive? Undoubtedly. From the beginning of mankind no substitute has ever been discovered. What shape it will take is impossible to describe at this time. How the Christian family will fare in an increasingly materialistic and hedonistic world will depend on the extent to which Christian parents follow the late Cardinal Suhard's advice: "We should live in this world in such a way that our life would not make sense if God did not exist." As members of the People of God groping in a new Diaspora, mothers and fathers might recall the words of Pius XII, who said that being loving and truly Christian parents calls for "a kind of bloodless martyrdom."

ON BECOMING A FAMILY

4

Simon Scanlon

If the family does not survive, there will be no social philosophers around to lament its passing. Hugh Hefner once made the profound revelation that, "without sex we would still be living in the caves." With all due respect to the Socrates of the Fold-out, the family played some part in getting us out of the caves, and, if it does not survive, we will wind up right back there in the caves. Since the family is the foundation of society, the other institutions had better do all they can to shore up the family if they themselves hope to survive. For, if the family goes down the drain, they will go with it.

We have much evidence that the family is in deep trouble at this point in history, most dramatically in the fifteen thousand teenagers who yearly gravitate to the Haight-Ashbury district and the Tenderloin of San Francisco. Those of us who contact these young runaways know that we are only picking up the pieces; we are not making any effective impact on the problem. The heart of the problem is evident from a typical situation in which one of the youths found himself.

One night a seventeen-year-old boy came into our coffee house and asked to talk to me. He said he had a problem. He was right.

Tom had gone through the standard routine of the runaway. He arrived in San Francisco with little money, unfinished education, no work experience. Having run away from home, he had no contacts in the business community. In a very short time he was broke, unemployed, and unemployable. He crash-padded with other young people in the same predicament for a while, but soon realized he had to have some source of income to survive.

There is just one establishment that was instituted to exploit the market of young dropout, inexperienced, unemployed, and unemployable runaway youths in San Francisco: the Meat Rack.

The Meat Rack is just what the words mean literally. There the young people are bought and sold as so much meat. The boys and girls stand in doorways or sit in all night hamburger heavens, on display like cuts of meat in a butcher shop, until an affluent homosexual or a pimp buys them. They survive, in a manner of speaking.

Prostitution or homosexuality entered into for economic reasons induces a deep self-hatred. To deaden the misery, to live with the self-hatred, the victims begin to use narcotics. This strengthens the grip of the pimps and other exploiters, assuring dependence on them for the narcotics and leaving the young people open to blackmail. You cannot support a narcotics habit as a bus boy or salesgirl in a department store, so the youngsters have to stay on the Meat Rack. But the going commodity on this Meat Rack, as on any other, is fresh meat; and you get old very young on the Meat Rack. This, together with a bumper crop of thirteen- to seventeen-year-old meat on the market, means that the runaways must then turn to car boosting, purse snatching, shoplifting, mugging and rolling drunks to survive.

Tom's problem was not unusual. A girl prostitute, who lived in the same dingy hotel as he, had been negotiating with two men. She had to go upstairs for some reason and she asked Tom to tell the men to wait for her, she would be back in a few minutes. Meantime another girl came along and began negotiation with the two men. Tom broke in on the conference and told the two customers that the first girl wanted them to wait. Soon two pimps approached Tom and told him that he had cost them two "tricks" (forty dollars) and that if he did not reimburse them before midnight they would take care of him. That meant a vicious beating at least, probably murder.

Of course, he did not want to go to the police. He had done some hustling and some petty thievery for the organization and was at their mercy. It took me about two hours to convince the boy that the only way out at the time was to go home, to get out of town.

I bought Tom's bus ticket for one of the best suburbs in Northern California. Just before boarding the bus, he turned to me and said, "In a way, I hate to go home. Here, for the first time in my life, I found people I could talk to about the most important things in my life, people who would listen to me and understand me."

This boy came from what we call one of our best suburbs, best neighborhoods, one of our best families, went to our best parochial grade schools and was a junior in one of our best Catholic high schools when he ran away. Why? Tom's answer was the one we hear over and over, in all kinds of circumstances, from the runaways: in that good family, good neighborhood, and good school and parish, he had not found community. He had run away and found an ersatz community: people like himself, not built into an organic true community but huddled together in a sleazy Tenderloin hotel through a common need and shared fear. Even this seemed better than no community at all.

Modern Jeremiahs have railed against white middle-class American families with much righteousness and gusto. They have blamed the parents for the demoralization of the young, for the breakdown of our society. While, from the vantage point of the human scrap heap of the Tenderloin, we can see that some of the complaints of the young and the charges of the Jeremiahs are valid, we can see, too, that the parents are as much victims as are the children of our time.

It is too true that we adults have given our youth examples of hypocrisy. They see people in their parents' circle make the promise "till death do us part" four or five times. They have seen a governor who ran on a platform of "Law and Order" call upon grade-school children to slash and steal tires of the school busses in order to prevent integration of the schools in compliance with the law of the land. The list of hypocrisies is too long to be recited here.

However, granting the bad example in high and low and middle places, the human limitations of this generation of parents, and the false standards our society has accepted, I believe that too much blame is attributed to parents. The odds against even the very best parents are just too great today. Too many of the other institutions of society are militating against the family for the family to function as it should.

A flood of pornography degrades the marriage relationship. And, even more widely harmful, television family situation comedies and commercials constantly portray the father, the head of the family, as a slob. Proposed new abortion laws, backed by physicians, would allow abortions without consulting the expectant father.

Women are exploited sexually to sell beer, deodorants, and cigarettes. They are used in business as dolls decorating an office. One unlamented television commercial for cigarettes presented a man, who resents this cigarette being made especially for women, throwing pies in the faces of attractive young women.

The word "economy" is a Greek root word that means, "the running of a household." We have come so far from the meaning of economics in our society that we gauge the health of the economy by the Dow Jones averages on the stock market. We should gauge it by the number of families that have adequate food, shelter, clothing, health care, education, and the means of taking part in cultural activities. Corporations deploy their employees as soldiers in battle, uprooting families and moving them about the country, keeping the head of the family "on the road" or spending so much time commuting that he becomes a weekend guest in his own home. Children with an absentee father see a parade of men on television or in movies who are either incompetent, effeminate slobs, or selfish, sadistic studs.

Until recently even the Church failed the family. Women were second-class citizens in the Church, marriage was thought of generally as an inferior state chosen by those who were not given a vocation to Religious Life or to the priesthood. Even women in Religious Life were treated as children, as witness that aging celibate males could make the decision as to what kind of clothing nuns would wear. The separate schools for boys and girls indicated a fear of the man/woman relationship.

For a long period in history the family was able to survive even with these factors militating against it. However, a situation has now developed that puts the family in an extremely hazardous position. There are certain bonds of community which previously worked *for* the family, which now not only do not function as bonds, but actually tend to disrupt community. The bonds of community are economics, recreation, education, and liturgy. All these social bonds should both reinforce and express the essence of community—mutual love.

In a more simple society, a rural society, such as we were before the twentieth century, economics united the family. The running of a household required that the father and the sons plow, till, and plant the soil, husband the livestock, and build and maintain the facilities of the home. The mother and daughters sewed and spun, cooked and preserved, and decorated the home. The very economy kept the members of the family in the home, forced them to cooperate with each other, to communicate with each other, and made them conscious of their interdependence on each other. The economy forged a bond within the family. This kind of economy also worked for community among neighbors. Families gathered together at harvest time to work together, or neighbors gathered to help build a home. This naturally moved into community recreation, such as harvest festivals, or neighbors coming to help put the roof on a home and staying to celebrate it. Even now, long after it has lost its economic meaning, a party is sometimes described as "raising the roof."

Today economics divides the family, scatters it rather than unites it. First, the economy demanded that the father leave the home in order to earn the means of supporting it. Then we accepted a standard of living and an economic system that took the mother out of the home to supplement the father's earning. Now, the economy is such that a recent survey showed that, in a big city, the average family moved eight times in seven years. That kind of "running of a household" not only divides the family unit but also prevents the family from growing any roots in a neighborhood, becoming part of a larger community. Should we wonder then that our children are rootless and restless? The economic bond has now been perverted into a force against the forging of community.

When the family was an economic unit it was also a social unit. Recreation was a bond of community. The family had to furnish its own recreation before radios and television. They would have community recreation: taffy pulling, apple ducking, singing together, reading aloud, telling stories, playing games, and telling riddles. They would pop corn, dye it, and save it to decorate the home for feasts. Coloring eggs, making candy, and presenting skits were recreations within the home. Hiking, picnicking, and picking berries were ways of sharing the beauties of nature together. Families gathered with other families at socials, picnics, and balls to create the larger community. All had the sense of belonging. In a song of the early century the singer tells us: "After the ball was over, after the dancers gone . . . a little maiden climbed an old man's knee, begged for a story, please Uncle do." The little maiden and the old man were at the ball. Now we have a "dance." Dances are segregated, held specifically for "teenagers," "young married," "young adults," "singles over thirty," or the like. Such events divide rather than unite. The family now parts for recreation: one to the golf course, one to a rock dance, one to the club, one to a bridge game. Or it sits at home, each oblivious of the others, hypnotized by the electronic eye or engrossed in sucking on a beer can or cocktail glass. Recreation is no longer a bond of community but a wall of separation. If you could persuade your parish or PTA or Lions Club to have a ball rather than a dance, you might keep some teenager off the Meat Rack, you might even be doing something to prevent World War Three.

In the simple society education began in the family. The parents had to teach the children the things necessary for the running of a household and for living in the larger community. As education became more specialized, the children left home for school. At first the school was small, a part of the community, and everybody knew that the school was an extension of the family, responsible to the family. Some schools had students from two, three, even four generations of one family. Now, with students moving eight times in seven years, the school is no longer a force for community, no longer can it give the sense of belonging. Separate schools for boys and girls, and for blacks and whites, not only broke the bond of education in the family but also built walls against coming together in the larger community.

With three of the four bonds of community now become walls of separation, the burden of rebuilding the community falls on the fourth, liturgy. Once, in primitive society, the home was the church. The father and mother taught morals and doctrine and the father conducted the simple liturgy of prayer and sacrifice. In recent history the liturgy had lost its psychological force for community. However, we must grant the Church one thing: she was the first of the institutions to see where she was failing and to criticize herself and to change.

That should have been a signal for the other institutions: business, communications, government, education, medicine, and the like to look at themselves and see where they were failing and where they must change. They did not. Rather, they all joined in to help the Church criticize herself. So, as of now, the Church bears the major part of the burden of sustaining and nurturing community in the family and the world.

The Church must eventually do more than she has done so far for the family. She must give women full membership, perhaps even the priesthood. Celibacy is a great dedication and a great witness. At one point in history, mandatory clerical celibacy saved the Church from simony and nepotism which were corrupting it. Maybe now, since the threats to the people of God are not simony and nepotism, but the crisis of the family and of the loss of community in all areas of life due to the loss of community in the family, another witness is needed. Perhaps now some diocesan priests are called to give witness by becoming the heads of Christian families. Perhaps a new kind of Religious Order, an Order which families join as families, is needed to save the world from going back to Hugh Hefner's caves.

The Church has begun its efforts to restore community to society at the point at which it must begin, at the family table of the people of God. The liturgy is now designed to be a community act. It gathers the family in the Father's House, to sing and learn and recreate and work and to grow in love. If the community is formed around this table it can give witness for community to the whole society. If people receive the sense of community there they can bring it to the institutions in which they function. They can make the world's family.

In the noncommunity in which I live and work there is much resistance to the new liturgy. The idea of community is alien to the minds of people here. They have been too long without it. We try to persuade the people but some are too set in their roles to change. We do, however, hope that we can prevent another generation from growing old alone. One Sunday I was trying to break down the walls of separation by explaining why the liturgy has been renewed. I asked the people to make just one expression of community: to hold the hand of the person next to them in the pew during the family prayer, the prayer to Our Father, taught to us by Our Brother, Jesus Christ.

Some people resisted, but others reached out to those who tried to withdraw. As I looked out over my brothers and sisters in the family of God, holding hands as they offered the prayer to Our Father, I was pleased—and then I was frightened. In only one pew did the occupants resist the effort for community. That group held my attention, and have never left my thoughts. The group that would not join hands was a natural family: a man, a wife, and two adolescent children, a boy and a girl. They were well-dressed, intelligent looking. The parents were so typical of those who come to our rectory or to the coffee house and show a picture of a good-looking teenager, and say: "I gave her everything . . . and yet she ran away and became a hippie . . . I heard that she is in San Francisco. Do you think you could try to find her?"

At the end of the book and film *Cool World,* someone asks the boy what became of the young fourteen-year-old girl who is the leading character in the story. He answers, "She got on a bus for San Francisco and nobody ain't heard of her since." It is hard for us here to find her among a crowd that grows by fifteen thousand each year. If that girl's family had learned to work together, learn together, play together, and pray together, she might still be at home.

THE TRANSITIONAL FAMILY

5

Eulah Laucks

Today, especially in the U.S., the disparity between where we are as human beings and where we are as technologists is so great, and the widening of the gap so rapid, that we are overwhelmed by cataclysmic dislocations in all areas of the culture. Moreover, the prospect for the future, whether or not we are all aware of it, is that we are likely to be living in a state of turmoil and disjunction for a long, long time. As has been said often enough, the impact of technology is cumulative, and nowhere is dislocation more apparent and more poignant than within the family, the traditional abode and source of humane and civilizing activity.

For better or for worse, people in this country now spend most of their waking hours in activities outside the home, and this scattering of interests and allegiances has weakened the family's capacity to take care of the increasingly crucial psychological needs of its members, let alone other needs. Added to that are changing attitudes toward women and their roles in public affairs. Woman is fast losing both image and actuality as the fixed and stable center of family activity.

In view of all this, when we are considering the likelihood of the family's surviving as a social unit, or when we are seeking methods for salvaging the family, reforming it, or envisaging its future, I think we must shake loose from the notion that the family is or should be a static entity, a structure inviolate and predictable that must persist in some constricted, encompassable form, essentially unchanged, without really basic reference to the radically changing environment. Not to put aside such fixed notions, sacrosanct as they have been in the past, is to burden the family with expectations borne of nostalgia for the good old days, and the next step, then, is to conclude that the traditionally structured family—and that only —can restrain or reorient a runaway technological society. This, I believe, is to be thinking backwards.

We cannot put the family back into a traditional box, "vacuum-packed," as George B. Leonard has so aptly put it. Nor can we hurry it into some utopian and equally static perfection. Like everything else, the family is likely to continue *evolving,* and, I believe, will not disappear, as some people predict. Now, more than ever, the family should be allowed to evolve *freely,* with the barest minimum of unavoidable restrictions, and certainly unencumbered by past theories of seemliness and old fears of losing our anchor to windward.

We might, however, cast one quick glance back, as much to discover what there may be good or bridge-building at the core of the family past, as to be done, once and for all, with our nostalgia. We should free ourselves from emotional attachments to the past, but we must be realistic about the fact that a part of the bridge to any future rests in the past.

Although in time we may come to discard the whole idea of the tight, little nuclear family—which Margaret Mead refers to as the "worst form ever invented"—we shall not soon get to the place where the act of love is not desirable; nor to the total efficacy of contraception; nor to the place where the human child will not need intimate care during its first years; nor to the total rejection of procreation by everybody. We can be sure that no utopian forms of the family will likely spring into being full-blown, or even partly blown.

Therefore, on the premise that some kind of family will persist, we might speculate that what is likely for the immediate future may be the development of diverse transitional forms. Certainly there are examples of such beginnings in some of the current experimental communities. I do not agree with predictions that the family will wither away altogether sometime in the next few decades, in spite of forecasts for the early 2000's of general artificial insemination, artificial lactation, extra-uterine gestation, and so on, which presumably will make anything now recognizable as family both unnecessary and undesirable except for small specialized units for the rearing of the humanoid remnants necessary for the survival of the species.

No, I believe that the idea and the actuality of the family will survive. Man has basic psychological and metaphysical needs that can be met only in some kind of authentic family structure. Of course, physiological sex drives, egoistic self-duplication drives, and the nurture needs of human infants may keep man partially familial during any future social upheavals or further technological advancements. Yet, he has deeper longings.

Even Marxists today—admittedly, sophisticated non-Stalinist Marxists—are acknowledging that man has ineradicable religious needs. I say that he also has ineradicable familial needs. He must *belong,* intimately. He has deep yearnings to express compassion, tenderness, and empathy, which can best be realized and released in responsibility for others who are closely dependent upon him. He has yearnings for continuity that stem from intimations of immortality to which the generation and nurture of children speak, as does the intimacy and belonging from which the desire to procreate and nurture spring in the first place. Further than that, man's innate recoil from chaos impels him to seek moorings. In the past, the family has been his refuge, and in spite of its present weaknesses, it will probably continue to be a refuge. However, it will have to widen its horizons so that it can become for all men the very source of fundamental human purpose.

Only in intimate community can the deeper longings of mankind find some fulfillment. Up to now, the only instrument providing hope of fulfillment of basic human needs has been the family. Therefore, in this time of aggravated alienation, it does not seem likely to suppose—even considering man's technology-deadened sensibilities— that he will discard the wellspring of whatever reciprocal love he has or can have for other human beings. Some form of family is man's very source of meaning.

Here we might ask: In this age of both easy contraception and overpopulation, what is it that should constitute the basic family form from which wider circles of community might grow? Man and woman alone (obviously children are no longer needed for economic or demographic reasons)? Man, woman, and one child (to provide emotional outlet and minimal renewal of the species)? Or, man, woman, and two children (to establish continuity of some kind with current patterns and perhaps look toward the population-controlled future)?

How about a transitional form that would stem from a blood-tied nucleus of man, woman, and offspring, and include a number of non-related people of any ages who just happen at a given time to live in the same vicinity, the same subdivision, the same block, or the same apartment building?

"Now that the survival of the race depends upon most couples having not more than two children," writes Mr. Leonard, "it becomes particularly important that we broaden the bonds of affection to include more than just spouse, children and pets."

Such family circles would not necessarily be fixed to place. Americans today have very little sense of place. Twenty percent have moved annually for the past 20 years. Half of the entire U.S. population does not live in its natal state. And in general, the whole world is in flux. What is needed is not fixity to place but fixity to a new consciousness of human need that can be transferred from place to place in a mobile society.

Within such transplantable transitional forms, no one family need be the central hub, except for itself. There might be a variety of familial nuclei, blood-related or not, radiating acceptance and community to and through one another in all modes and directions within a given area. Depending on the length and strength of such radiations, there need be no particular restrictions as to space. Thus it might be hoped that eventually even national boundaries might be encompassed and overreached and the world community so much desired by so many people might have its beginning.

The idea of family extension in purely blood-tie terms has exhausted itself for our age. Along with whatever benefits and virtues it may have had for times past, it also gave rise to some of the worst evils that have plagued us—elitism, suspicion, fear, competition, and greed—the continuance of which offers hope to no part of the world today. Further than that, when one considers how few people—especially in this country—now have all, many, or any of their relatives living near them, the idea of blood-tied extended families becomes rather academic anyway.

If we can change our attitudes sufficiently to tolerate the idea of strangers as members of our families—more from acceptance of them as fellow people in newly forming communities than as strangers complicating our lives—transitions would not be so hard to come by. What is needed as a beginning, of course, is a deliberate effort to accept the idea of new, radical approaches to the possibilities available.

I think the actual process of widening family circles must in some way come about spontaneously. There should be no selecting out of people for one's own benefit, by age, sex, occupation, hobbies, or other categories, in the manner of forming associations or private clubs. This is the revolving door back to constriction and elitism.

The trend toward dispersal of in-groups into ever smaller and more exclusive units and especially into peer groups, has reached a high mark today. It seems to me notable that this separation of people coincides roughly with age groupings. We have subdivision after subdivision designed especially for the young marrieds, where there is no room in their tight little split-level boxes for grandparents, aunts, and uncles. We have "leisure" complexes for the care and feeding of the retired old, where their lives can be carefully prolonged in isolated uselessness. We have phalanxes of manicured apartment buildings for the childless and petless, who are mostly middle-aged. To a large extent, these segregations have been the cause of not one but several kinds of generation gap, the like of which could not have been predicted even twenty years ago.

Perhaps future man, concentrating as he will be on fiddling with the Universe, will be relatively unaffected by such separations and gaps. I could better believe it if he were not now also separated or institutionalized into ever larger and larger groups of the mentally ill, the alcoholic, the drugged, and the criminal.

I feel that dispersal of human persons into isolated units will have to end. New, humane, open-sided aggregations of people must come into being that will tend toward ever-expanding circles of cooperation and unity. For a long while, such new family circles probably will have to be transitional and experimental. The crucial need is for radical change in *attitudes* in order that fundamental acts in the direction of human transcendence will take place, rather than makeshift or ill-intended renovations of the materialism that has been degrading us.

It is true, of course, that dispersal has brought us awareness (through mobility and communication) of the unified structure of the planet and the limit of its space, but it has so far failed to make clear that we are not random pieces to be flung apart in all directions, but valuable parts of a whole that should have an overall unity of purpose. To help find that purpose should be an important function of the transitional family.

How, then, can we encourage expansions of the family that will take in nearby strangers, close our proliferating generation gaps, retain a sense of belonging while at the same time allow for our mobile, dispersed modes of living today? We can no more easily live in tight little planetary neighborhoods than we can in nuclear families that revolve around themselves. We ache for the *Lebensraum* of the world and we are not prepared psychologically to share it with ever-increasing concentrations of strangers. Our present inclination is to insulate ourselves and our loved ones against the encroachment of the world, or to flee with them to wildernesses we dream are still available but know neither exist nor would be tolerable to us now if they did. There is no help but to be friends with strangers, and we must extend the idea of family to include them in ever larger numbers.

We are one big family in our crowded earth house. Sooner than we may think we will have to find out how to live together peaceably, and if possible, joyfully. This will require new definitions of family and radical changes in attitudes toward the meaning and purpose of family. It will mean there will have to be radical changes in thinking about the fundamental purpose of human existence. If we can lead ourselves by our familial needs into acting on ideas about communal living, we may in time discover fortuitously what this fundamental purpose is.

I suggest letting the family create itself in diverse, transitional forms, in the hope that, given freer rein, it may not only evolve into a means for closing the chasm between man's present retarded wisdom and his technological expertise, but will eventuate in a purer vision of what life is all about. I feel strongly that the evolution of the family today must be a free-flowing and natural development. I do not see how we can deliberately plan or design or invent forms into which to fit or force it for the future. It seems to me that in the very act of manufacturing a form, as if it were some kind of product, we would destroy the freedom of its evolution, and hence the likelihood of its viability. I think transitional family forms must ensue as a consequence of changed attitudes toward available possibilities and not *vice versa*. That is to say, not as the result of our designing fixed structures to try out and manipulate into workability.

We can, perhaps, do something about providing environments which will aid the development of family inclinations. In writing about needs for our survival and salvation today, Robert L. Heilbroner points out that we must find ways to rebuild our cities so that urban living will again become tolerable. It seems obvious that not in any foreseeable, crowded, technological interim can we expect an appreciable outflow of people from central ghettos. Therefore, we must somehow remake or rehabilitate these areas for a long transitional pull. We must orient such efforts toward allowing new family groupings to form. James Reston wrote recently, "The more the rising generation has to live in crowded cities . . . the more it is going to have to depend on the family . . ." Of course, whether or not we can refashion the central cores of our cities—even if only temporarily—according to preconceived designs, and at the same time allow the necessary freedom for the formation of *diverse* transitional family forms, remains a hard question. However, it seems to me that if these islands of miserable humanity could witness and take part in action that would provide real hope for a changed existence, they might be sufficiently inspirited to be catalyzed into all kinds of spontaneous activity from which new ideas about family and community might grow and form.

At this point it may be asked: Is there a priority of principles upon which family formations must be based? In order to come to an adequate understanding of the importance of the family to humanity, much more and deeper research must be done to uncover and define the essence of the yearning experience people of all races and creeds have *in their guts* when the term "family" is used. If this could be clarified and brought to acceptance in the practical world, we could begin at least with a flat, unassailable assertion that the *family* is basic to human purpose.

If this assertion were accepted as fact, the present trend toward suspicion and denigration of the whole notion of family worth might be turned into a search for ways to nurture and encourage into palpability the stuff out of which the family of the future might develop.

If I were to name the elements necessary for the formation of authentic family substance, I would begin not with sex—as necessary as it is—but with friendship. Friendship demands not only vulnerability but an act of faith. Emphasis on friendship is not unfitting, either, if we insist that the nuclear family must expand itself to include strangers in ever-widening circles. To most people, the mention of family suggests a place where one is comfortable. To be "at home," to be "in the bosom of one's family," is to be enveloped in friendship of the highest order. The family, of course, can become closed and turned in on itself, even if strangers are included. This is what has nurtured, not cooperation, but the deadly competition we have today. Transitional forms, at some points in their development, may have to go through phases of elitism, of course, but the constant bearing must be toward nonexclusivity and openness. This is why the extended family should not be deliberately planned to include only people of like interests, race, age, economic status, and so on. There should be randomness in the make-up, homogeneity only in ideals and purpose. There must be no deliberate channeling or manipulation.

If, then, a first principle of the family is friendship, another non-exclusivity and a third heterogeneity, a fourth might be educative responsibility. The family must be a vital source of education. If, as Robert M. Hutchins says, our future society can be a "learning society" wherein there is educative experience for everybody, the family must take back its part of the educative function that it has given over to the schools. It must discard the false belief that the schools can do its educative job better. A whole new idea of education must come into being. Transitional educative forms must evolve side by side with transitional family forms and be intimately related to them. Recognizing that there is dignity and purpose in the human person, we should realize the fallacy of trying to run people through schooling processes with the same techniques we use for the mass production of disposable merchandise. It is time to reconsider doing the job by hand, in the family and elsewhere.

We should be able to get some ideas from the Brazilian educator, Paulo Freire, whose approach is to take people, particularly adults, "where they are," at any age or state of learning, and bring them to literacy by way of their current needs and interests. Thus, they are given the chance to decide for themselves what they want to know about the world and their places in it. By such methods, education becomes an integral part of people's daily living, in the family and in the community. I consider this imperative.

If the family is to survive and again become an influential and acculturative unit of society, the activities of family, community, and the educative process must be coherent. What happens in the family must be intimately related to what happens in the community at large. The education of the young and the continuing learning of the elders cannot take place, as unrelated processes, apart, largely disconnected from family grouping, but must take place within the inseparable sphere of home and community, providing coherent educative experience for everybody.

Educative responsibility, then, is another indispensable part of family substance. The internal diversity of transitional family forms

—of all sizes, shapes, and colors—outwardly functioning with regard for the evolving tastes and activities of society, might supply fertile ground for the learning society of the future.

Another consideration that bears on basic principles is the necessity for doing something about the limitation of offspring. Mr. Leonard states: "Perhaps it's true that our distant past as hunters required fast breeding, with lasting pair-bonding to assure care for our slow-maturing young. Now, these tendencies work against us, creating overpopulation . . ."

If demographers are correct, nothing short of a widespread plague or nuclear decimation will save the planet from a state of standing room only within the lifetimes of our youth today. Whatever is done about population control, however, the prerogative of voluntary procreation must remain. As in the case of dictated family forms, the good we would have happen is not likely to happen except through the freedom to choose. This involves education, and since time is of the essence, highly innovative education.

The enumeration of basic principles would be incomplete without some reference to the religious or metaphysical roots of family formation. In order to foster new attitudes toward transitional forms, we might create, or disinter from the depths of history, some viable myths (not ideologies) that will reinforce by faith or intuition the logic of the family. Such myths will not be found in the solidified and encrusted layers of the immediate past where lie our fearful affinities to rigid patriarchal or matriarchal authority. I think they will be found, if at all, either at the deepest levels of some remote past or in the gropings of today's young for a different kind of society, in both of which places the dignity and freedom of the human person is likely to take precedence over all other considerations.

We might pause here to wonder about the innovative philanthropies of young millionaires like Stewart Rawlings Mott (heir to General Motors money) who apparently have rejected the self-centered notions on which their fortunes were built and the belief that family and the building of great capitalistic empires have interlocking purposes. Although present intentions of these young men to use their wealth to help less fortunate people and to make things right with the world may diminish or fade away—and even if their actions may stem from a mixture of altruism and personal ambition—they have excited into imagination all kinds of new possibilities for the common good of the future.

If the common good includes the necessity for peace, the transitional family must be one in which, in the words of Gloria Steinem, "sex roles are clear but not polarized." She suggests that the "male-female role-playing problem" is probably the greatest threat to peace. She says that anthropologists have found that the few societies without war have been those in which sex roles have been clearly delineated but not polarized. Neither patriarchal nor matriarchal rigidities should have any place in the evolution of the family of the future. The female dropouts from hippie communities have often been the result of the prevalent male assumption that women members should "make coffee, not policy."

I think an unbiased study has yet to be made of the effect of the hippie communes on the development of the idea of family. Most hippie groups are highly experimental, and more than will be admitted are escapist without positive aspirations for mankind. Yet, many authentic families may be forming among them that are adhering to universal principles of community. Dr. B. F. Skinner, Harvard psychologist, says hippie communities are too poorly organized to survive, but he predicts that before the end of the century Americans will start a trend toward communal living.

Where many well-intentioned hippie communities fail, I believe, is in their communal sharing, not only of trust, comradeship, material benefits, child care, play, and so on, but in sharing genital union. Although we cannot rule this out altogether for the future, I think it will be some time before we are ready for the exchange of genital sex *en masse*. Probably many waves of transition will have to occur before complete freedom of sexual exchange can be included in on-going family forms. Statistics seem to indicate that communal genital union is likely to lead to cultish hierarchies that become predominantly patriarchal, hence possessive and manipulatory. Since we usually destroy what we dominate, many of these developments are short-lived. Transitionally, they are not very helpful, since they project little that is solid enough to be walked upon for passage into the future.

How much affectionate bodily contact short of genital sex can be carried on among people in community without compromising the interchange of authentic friendship remains to be determined. Many sensitivity and "encounter" groups today function on the premise that transcendence of the human spirit can be attained only through freeing the physical senses of acculturated inhibitions. This seems to be a basic tenet of youth today, also. One thing can be said for this attitude: its emphasis on the human need for simple *joyfulness* is something we lack abysmally today. I am afraid we also lack the capacity to deeply and unselfishly cherish anything. Perhaps we should place at the top of the list of first principles for the family a strong desire for its survival.

We must tolerate and then learn to love the enveloping world we have made for ourselves, and we must learn to live in it with human dignity and brotherhood. Thus, we may be able to accept the ultimate in planetary thinking; the unitary nature of humanity on the planet, Earth. If the significance of today's instant communication and jet mobility has not fully penetrated our consciousness, the awesome pictures of our planet from space should convince us that the whole world has broken into the family circle and is not likely to retreat. Therefore, the family must let down its bulwarks and in diverse and transitional ways let in the world, in ever-widening circles, until the point arrives in the process of evolving culture when there will be only one great earth-girdling circle, around the family of man.

FAMILY

6

Sidney Callahan

There are few absolutes left anymore, but one remains: the family is necessary for the survival of man. As a species human beings must have air, water, food, shelter, and a family system of some sort. If the family does not survive, then neither do we.

There is simply no substitute for what the family does. No culture has ever survived without a family structure and it is inconceivable that man in the future could function without the family. This is not to say that there will not be many variations and transformations of the family, indeed the whole culture will change vastly; but no change outside of the improbable conquest of death can make the family outmoded.

As long as man dies, new people will be needed to replace every generation. Man comes into the world as a newborn, even if he should be fertilized and nurtured in a glass uterus for nine months. Since man is the most complex, most rational, and most emotional of any known species, there is no way to get from newborn to adult without the sustained, emotionally involved, continuous care of adult human beings. No machine, no computer, can love or laugh or respond appropriately in speech. More obviously, no machine can provide bodily contact with an adult human being.

Moreover, since sexual differentiation is genetically sound and aesthetically and emotionally appealing it is probably here to stay despite technology. Thus a newborn needs the experience of love and care from the two sexes while maturing, in order to prepare him or her for a sexed world. While there remains a social difference in the sexual roles it is even more important for a child to experience intimately the lives of at least one man and one woman. More normally at least two intimately known adults give a child more than a single access to adult life; two parents can be a corrective, one to the other. Two parents, in addition to supporting each other, also serve as better insurance in case of the death of one.

A basic form of the family emerges from these reflections on the biological situation of man. Basically, each human individual needs a minimum of two concerned committed adults, preferably of two sexes, who will provide a continuous care and help in the transition from helplessness to adulthood. Continuity of care is important from early stages on in order to establish emotional involvement and excellent cognitive functioning. Early, object constancy and the ability to abstract require a cognitive understanding of the world based on continuity of environment. Since other people are primary in our environment, we must as infants and more importantly, as toddlers, have a few constant people and as constant an environment as possible.

The great work done in the last fifty years on cognitive development by such giants as Piaget and other such investigators of language acquisition as Bruner and Brown, reveal the need for consistent adult initiation of the child into language and thought. While more may be innate and inherent in the species than the early empiricists dreamed, still it takes other adult humans to release it. The idea of environmental releasers has relevance for the family. Adults in the family release and facilitate speech, for instance, by expanding and correcting the child's attempts. The child learns from this on-going dialogue and picks up all the complicated rules from hearing the language spoken.

If no adult is continuously around talking and caring for him, however, the child's development is stunted. Part of the deprivation of ghetto children has been the absence of sustained conversation and continuous care. Language development is an index and pre-requisite to intellectual growth. Even before language acquisition, however, there is a preverbal dialogue with the caretaker which sustains life and initiates the child into the world. Patterns in asking and giving, discomfort and relief, passivity and stimulation are formed by the caretaker's reading of the signals and cues in the infant. The "dialogue" sustains life.

Children who are physically ignored die. Children who are phys-ically cared for but who are not given consistent care and individu-alized stimulation in an emotional dialogue can be severely retarded or, in severe cases, also die. Survival in man is not just a biological process. A bond must be formed with others in order to live. Fami-lies make care, stimulation, and the bond possible for the young.

Every institution that has had to replace the biological family for one reason or another, has found an imitation of the basic form of the family to be the most effective policy. Foster families have replaced the large institution in which large groups of children are placed together with changing shifts of adults. Homes for delinquent or retarded children, homes for mentally ill children (and adults) have developed the family structure as a therapeutic measure. A man, a woman (preferably married as a couple) live together with their small group of dependents needing care. Even the older chil-dren in the kibbutzim children's houses often have a male teacher and a female caretaker assigned to them, supplementing their daily time with parents.

The crucial factor in the reconstruction of families as a therapeutic measure seems to be the limited number of people that can be re-lated to on an intense and deep level. Adults can rarely manage rela-tionships with extended numbers of people, and apparently children can manage even fewer ties. Some anthropologists have postulated that man as a species is basically a small group organism and will always find clusters of people more compatible than vast numbers.

Be that as it may, immature children without developed perceptual systems or strong identities need a few familiar caretakers to be sustained in their growing identities. The bond of love also allows the child to react against the adult and test himself. The family is needed to insure a healthy amount of conflict and aggression. Nothing is more distressing than the "good" passive behavior often found in institutionalized groups of children.

From the child's point of view then, the family fulfills a basic biological and social need. Food, warmth, care, clothing, and surveillance to insure air and medical attention give biological life. Merging and emerging from these biological needs for caretaking we see psychogenic needs that are also fulfilled in a normal family environment.

The emotional aura surrounding the caretaking process is conveyed by stroking, hugging, kissing, and vocal endearments. Language and physical proficiency seem to flourish when the child is given a lot of affection and attention, both physical and verbal. Intelligence develops from the child's observations of adults and from adult observations of the child. Long-term, intense familiarity allows the observer to figure things out about the other party. Adapting and adjusting to another person is a mutual enterprise that is basic to interpersonal relationships for the rest of life. Tactlessness and gross insensitivity to people begins in the crib.

Body image and one's attitude toward one's body also begins in infancy and childhood. Aversion to bodily functions can be conveyed to the child by the caretaker, or a healthy acceptance which imposes limitations only for social reasons of hygiene and comfort. Confidence and self-acceptance begin in the family. Later sexual attitudes and sexual competence can be influenced by the pleasures of human contact as a child. Whatever the details of the so-called family romance, surely children do learn to love and desire those nearest and dearest to them where they have been loved first. Man seems naturally to love what is familiar, so family life prepares for adult love life in a very direct way.

Cognitive style and cognitive functioning are also nurtured by the family. Each of us has a characteristic way of figuring things out and going at problems. We learned much of that in early days when "the small scientist" in the crib goes to work figuring out the world. Apparently each child goes through a gradual process of mental development in ordered stages. However, within the norms of growth there are endless variations arising from individual difference.

Dr. Sybil Escalona, a noted authority in child development, has done a fascinating study of the individual differences in babies. The response to varied stimuli differs from child to child so that different patterns of stimuli are needed to arouse different children. Since one function of caretaking is to protect from too much stimuli, different patterns of protection are also needed for different children so they are not overwhelmed. A bouncy super-social baby may easily get frantic when overstimulated socially, while a quiet impassive baby needs coaxing and lengthy stimulation to respond at all.

Families can provide the context for adapted stimulation and protection from overstimulation. A unique child, as each child is, can be attended to and adjusted to by those who know him best and are willing to go to the trouble over a long-term period. Since the needs of a growing child keep changing from stage to stage, new adjustments are constantly needed on the part of caretakers. Yet often the previous experience of an earlier period helps in dealing with a new stage of growth. Familiarity with a personal style can help in understanding and guiding a growing person.

While much has been done in emotional and cognitive development, less has been done in studying the moral development of children. Undoubtedly, moral development exists like other kinds of development with norms and variations from the norm according to individual differences. The family context helps here in many ways. Rules and guiding principles are conveyed overtly and explicitly, and also, of course, implicitly through the behavior of the parents. The earliest lessons of the child in moral behavior are surely in the way he was treated when he was a helpless dependent.

While Freud's idea of the father's role in the development of the superego is easily dismissed, the existence of loving people who care and will disapprove, when necessary, is indeed all-important in moral development. The family makes real the abstract idea of a community and an external reality that must be taken into account and served. Other people become real in the small group context of childhood experience. Ties to these people facilitate ties to humanity in general. A feeling of secure belonging in family life can produce a secure belonging adult who feels that *his* society is worth personal sacrifices to preserve. This sense of belonging and security is probably more formative than any form of punishment used in child-rearing.

As a society becomes more mobile and fragmented the individual nuclear family becomes more important in giving a sense of being a part of humanity. Without clan or tribe or commune or extended family the burden of belonging falls to the parents and siblings. Parents have to make up for a lack of ancestor worship, a totem, and a divine myth of origin. All of the things that have helped give man a sense of at-homeness in the world are concentrated in the two parents. They must stand in for the "cloud of witnesses" that have observed ethical decisions through the ages. They must be able to convey that citizenship in the universe is worth the effort. Concern for the species and the future of man begins to a certain degree in the child's acceptance of his origins and his family's ability to make the future desirable.

Family life is not just for children. Adults benefit from family life too. Many have noted, along with Erik Erikson, that the fulfilled adult life enters a generative stage. After developing one's self and making it to successful adulthood and intimacy with another, there naturally arises a desire to generate a future. The adult wishes to care for others, to give as he has been given to, to assure a future to his people and his community. Adulthood gravitates to the thankless tasks of keeping the world going, whatever that means in that culture.

One channel for this ripening of generosity in man is, of course, the family. Children provide the simplest means to give and love, teach and initiate, care for and develop other persons. All one's fantasies from one's own childhood of being the strong, good, loving parent can be enacted in adulthood. The joy of watching a baby and then a young child and young adult develop pervades family life. The future is at hand in family life. No one is out of touch when in the middle of the demands of growing children.

Even the difficulties, distresses, and sadnesses of family life provide challenge and growing room for the adult. Man does not just seek tension release and the easiest course. There is something in us all that relishes the struggle, the effort, the problem to solve. Coping with children and caring for them provides these less obvious satisfactions. Rising to meet the complex challenge of responsibility for the small group, we become more than we were alone.

Erikson has expressed the effect of childrearing on adults in a very witty way. "Every baby raises his parents," says he, "while the parent raises his child." Could one say that you get the parents you deserve? Probably not, but the idea that childrearing is a two-fold learning process should be strongly stressed. Here again, the intimacy and the pressure of absolute commitment makes conflict inevitable. The person who can say that he or she has never hated anyone has obviously never raised a child to adulthood. Childrearing conflicts give the adult self-knowledge as no other situation possibly can. Illusions about one's self are dispelled in family life. As one is threatened by the stress and strain of childbearing, one gets new insights and learns to cope and give in many new dimensions of personality and life.

In later life after one has learned to give and give and take family responsibility, the opposite qualities are called for. Parents have to learn at the end to let go, give up, and finally, receive. Attention must be withdrawn from the family and the couple realigned toward the community at large. This prepares for the final state of old age when dependency becomes a central problem again. Families then can provide the shelter and cushion against overwhelming stimuli as capacities to cope narrow under the stress of disease and age. The support of a family is important in dying well. A lonely death and anonymous burial has seemed a human tragedy in most cultures. To be cared for and mourned while dying is a confirmation of one's life. "I have been a part of the human community, I reap what I've sown."

Basically the family gives a person a field in which to sow and reap, cultivate and grow, and struggle and rest. On an intimate scale and in a unique individual context, a family allows a development of life style and a testing of powers. One's family is a shelter from the larger community and a launching ground for reentry into a less intimate world. We get both refuge and the most intimate challenges to self within the family context. It is the absolute quality of the family commitment which taps deep currents of personality. Biologically, the family is an irreversible relationship. The irreversibility of the family relationship has been both the source of conflict and the source of the security and satisfaction for man.

However, I have been careful in my argument so far to avoid arguing only biologically, since I think the basic form of the family is not dependent upon blood relationship. The essential element is the irreversible commitment that has usually been correlated with physical procreation and blood ties. Yet since man is cultural and cognitive as well as biological, the basic irreversible tie can be one of will and desire rather than blood. Indeed, in marriage the couple found a family without previous kinship ties. They leave one family in order to form a new family. The universal incest tabu is a break with one's nearest kin.

In the same way the biological family can give way to or be supplemented with the family of choice or will or commitment. Adoption is as old as human culture. It is a basic model for all future extensions of the family. My contention is simply stated. We must have family to survive as a species, but we can extend the family and transform the biological family if the essentials are retained. I have already discussed the essentials: Two adults of different sexes, irreversible commitment to insure continuous loving care and initiation into human culture.

I see the extension of the family occurring in two ways: One through technology; the second through social change that will innovate and reinstate other ways of family life. Technology is much less interesting to discuss. All sorts of medical miracles await us in the future. Genetic engineering, intervention in every stage of conception and gestation, new processes of birth and lactation are just on the horizon if not already developed. The ethical and legal aspects to these developments are enormous but they do not have much to do with family life. No matter where the baby came from and what tinkering has been done in the biological processes, family life begins with the helpless infant and the adults who are going to rear him. The commitment of these adults to this child must be irreversible, so everything that technology can do must not disturb this end result.

Here the special case of the single adult who is alone with his or her child merits some attention. Either through desertion, divorce or through adulterous conception, adoption or through death, a parent can find himself in the special family situation of being a single parent. One parent is preferable to none, although two parents are a basic norm that should be seen as an ideal. Hopefully, social changes and extensions of family life which will develop can alleviate this difficult situation. One of the first changes might be the downgrading of lineage considerations, and an increased emphasis upon love, responsibility, and commitment. No child should have to suffer because of his origins; "bastard" can disappear as a term from our vocabulary forever, no child can be called "illegitimate" legitimately.

Other social changes that will benefit all families would be some recognition and support from the community at large for families. Child allowance plans, regardless of the status of the parents, would be a start in the right direction. Family allowances, family health care, family education, family support, all sorts of unremarkable measures every other advanced country considers a minimum, could surely be instituted in the U.S. Since the new generation is the most precious resource a country possesses, it makes sense not to starve, freeze, deprive, undereducate, or poison children. Sowing so much neglect and oppression of children and their families, America prepares a bitter harvest in the future.

The problem, however, is not one just found in the deprived section of our country. Middle-class affluent groups also need developments in family life. The lack of legislation reflects a lack of support for family life in general. I see a great need for support for the extended family, for a development of new forms of extended family life, and education and sensitizing of the culture to family values. This becomes all the more vital because the population crisis is upon us, and there will have to be fewer and fewer children born. Culturally, we must devise ways to share the children and share in family life without increasing the birth rate. We are faced with the interesting challenge of becoming a child-centered, family-centered culture with anti-natal goals. Can we be against births and for children?

First, how can we support the extended family system which, contrary to some reports, is anything but dead in this country? Many, many Americans would gladly share more in extended family relationships if they could. In the case of older parents, and older aunts and uncles, the problem seems basically one of housing and transportation. Old-age benefits can take care of subsistence and medical payment plans can take care of medical problems, but the psychogenic needs to belong and yet be independent revolve around housing and a good transportation system (maybe free?). Older people do not wish either to live with their children or in institutions filled with diseased and dying peers. Some way can be found to build housing units that avoid isolation from community and family. The generation gap on the other end of the life cycle is also crucial.

In addition to supporting the extended family system, we must devise new ways of extending the family. Many people cherish the freedom to leave their biological family. Many people through necessity must leave all family behind them. Many people have been deserted by their families or come from families broken by death, divorce, or disease. These people still need the support of family life. If they are single they need a small group in which to belong and be able to give and receive. If they are married and childless they can enjoy ties with other couples and their children, or with older people or single people. Those engaged in raising families themselves most need support in family life.

For families engaged in family life, I envision the encouragement and increasing of guilds or movements of families banding together for support and stimulation. The clan fulfilled a need that an association of families could meet. The Christian Family Movement has been a model for the kind of growing, friendships, and commitments that can be produced in groups of families. Something more dramatic might be developed through sharing summer quarters, as many rich families have always done informally, or perhaps, by buying an apartment house and experimenting with cooperative ventures while retaining family autonomy.

For another group even more experimentally inclined, a more fully communal life together as a family can be lived. Sharing economically while eating and living together allows ties to be forged that are as strong as kinship. Most communes in history have foundered if sexuality was shared too, but with approximate, agreed-upon monogamy, the commune can be a satisfying and prospering way to live. After all, communities of celibate monks have shown through the centuries the advantages of a life where all share work in friendship.

Christian communal life, though, including some groups of families and married couples, has usually required a great deal of conformity. Common ideals and a common social life and often a common vocation have been the price for community. The interesting new development is the attempt to have a communal family life of adoption that is not so rigidly conformist.

It seems particularly good for the children in an adopted family to have access to more adults and vice versa. Childless people in such a "family" can share in the joys and problems of childrearing while children can know adults well. Again, as in monogamy, the child must belong to somebody specifically, but he can be shared and enlarged by other adult relationships in a small loving group. In the old extended family residing together, the uncle and aunt relationship was a precious one. Commune members can recreate that with the family's children. The children can have a sibling or cousin relationship with each other. With small families becoming a necessity, children too can be deprived of knowing many children intimately.

New forms of adoption and godparenthood can increase ties between the generations. Could you adopt a grandparent? Or could you get a tax reduction for sponsoring a child and helping his family to support and educate him? More sharing of children and grandparents could be encouraged by letting an adult in free to events if he is accompanied by a child or senior citizen. Similarly, other problems of the lonely aged could be alleviated by encouraging their participation in mainstream events by economic incentives. Common residence is not the only way to foster extended family relationships.

None of these things can come about unless we become sensitive as a culture and a people to the importance of family values. If we do not teach child development and family life courses in school, we are missing an opportunity to sensitize a generation to core concerns. Apprentice programs in child care and family living could help youngsters to gain more experience than they can get from their own particular family background. Concern for the aged can come with increasing attention to their problems, urged on perhaps by the power of our elders' ballot.

Study of the human life cycle may be stimulated by the whole burgeoning interest in ecology which at the very least is an effort to see man restore harmonious relationships with himself and his environment. When man becomes conscious of himself as a species, he cannot ignore the unique necessity of family in his biological survival and enculturation. A revival of family studies, and family legislation and family experimentation may be on the way in the seventies. We may be seeing just the beginning of the ascendance of the family as a self-conscious organism, rather than questioning whether the family can survive.

COMPUTERS, COMPATIBILITY, AND COMMUNITY

7

William Bishop

Man, the toolmaker, has probably applied every product of his in-genuity to the task of matchmaking at one time or another. If we can believe the cartoonists, the caveman used his dinosaur club to facilitate his courting of the fair sex, and melodrama villains of the Snidely Whiplash variety have long used the buzz-saw to convince the heroines of their invincible charm. The shotgun has been such an effective tool in the promotion of accelerated courtship that it has given its name to a special wedding ceremony, while the influ-ence of the automobile on courting practices is well known, or, at least, is widely suspected. The computer is now taking its place in this honorable tradition and in doing so has raised the technology of courtship into a position of overwhelming superiority over the technology of marriage.

In promising to find for each and every one of us a highly com-patible partner ("as nearly compatible as is possible to modern technology") our electronic mentor is virtually guaranteeing that there will be a continuous stream of couples headed for the altar, or the point of embarcation of their choice. But even in the present state of the art, far more people are getting married than can ever stay married. In fact, marriage has become one of the most popular tourist attractions of our time. One no longer takes out a license in order to enter the state of matrimony; he merely requests a visa. Like many places that have been discovered by the heavy tourist trade, marriage has been spoiled for many of the most discerning. Those who might once have found marriage a nice place to visit but would not want to live there, have begun scouting around for some other state in which to enjoy their blessed compatibility.

What about that term "compatibility"? It seems to have a slightly metallic overtone when it is applied to the description of the relations between a man and a woman. One can more easily understand its appropriateness when speaking of the compatibility of mass-produced machine parts—particular parts that are cut to the same pattern and are interchangeable. A pair of machine gears is an excellent example of compatability; when they are placed side by side and their teeth are engaged, they move in perfect harmony. No, not in perfect harmony, for harmony implies a certain depth and feeling of mystery that can never be present in the relationship of one machine gear to another. Compatibility is a much better term for the gears, at least until one of them begins to wear a bit. When that happens the profile of the gear begins to soften and it does not engage the other so sharply. Perhaps a tooth breaks and when the empty spot on the gear turns to that point at which it should engage the other gear it has no way of taking hold and is left motionless as the other gear turns on. Thus, the end of compatibility calls for replacement.

Why, then, have we come to use such a term to describe inter-personal relationships? I think this question will lead us to consider one of the significant ways in which our view of ourselves is affected by our technology.

There is a very widely shared feeling that our technological process has somehow become an autonomous movement and is no longer under the control of those who manage it. This is most deeply felt when the question of its effect on our natural environment is under consideration or when one makes the attempt to sort out the meaning of certain technological priorities. Why, for example, is it more important to pour our resources into the development of parking spaces on the moon than to engage these resources in the development of a life-sustaining environment in our cities? We often try to explain the difficulties involved in such questioning by telling ourselves that our material technology has far outdistanced our moral means to order our affairs. This idea that technology and morality constitute two separate and competing fields of expertise has such a strong hold on our minds that one of the most popular images of today's editorial cartoonist is that of the caveman wielding an atomic club: primitive moral mentality in possession of an incredibly sophisticated weapon of destruction. Somehow, we have come to believe, moral gadgetry has not kept pace with technological gadgetry. The fairly recent arrival of a new and, presumably, improved morality probably will not alter that belief very much, though it may serve to reinforce the idea that morality is indeed a form of gadgetry and that it actually is in some sort of race with technology.

There is a basic confusion here and it concerns the old problem of ends and means. Technology is a process and morality is a system of values. The technological process is the means which we employ to supply our material needs and to overcome our material limitations. Morality is a system of values that should determine the ends toward which we will move and should also stand in judgment over the means that will be employed in the pursuit of those ends. I say *should* because there is never any guarantee that we will exercise the kind of moral judgment that is called for and because there is plenty of evidence that we can become so hypnotized by the cleverness of our means and so dependent on the material results of those means that we quite forget to exercise moral judgment over them. In the resulting moral vacuum, values which have sprung up within the process itself take over control and become free from "outside" influence. Efficiency, for example, is one of the guiding concepts within the process and its value there is so overwhelming that it can become a pseudomorality in itself.

Thus, morality is outdistanced by technology not through any lack of advance in moral concepts but by our refusal to bring moral considerations to bear on the ends to be pursued and the means to achieve those ends.

The cult of efficiency has enjoyed such success within the material process that it was inevitable, in a society which so admires success, that it should move into other areas and even into the area of interpersonal relations. There it is translated into the term which we were considering before: *compatibility,* the manifestation of efficiency in personal relations.

Compatibility has long been both glue and lubricant in dealing with the problems of industrial personnel. The necessity of holding people together and assuring that they work productively together called for the development of the specialized field of human relations in an industrial situation. Where relationships are not a matter of personal choice some pattern of expectations has to take the place of personal intimacy. People who must work together whether they like it or not had best find some way of disliking it as little as possible. A pattern of responsibilities and expectations that eliminates special privilege and antagonistic forms of competition may enable personnel to function well together even though the persons involved might not choose to come together on their own time. A person might fit with complete compatibility into his niche at work and then seek psychological comfort at home in the exercise of his own type of eccentricity; moving from a pattern of essentially external relationships at work to a pattern of intimacy at home.

We are such a dynamic nation of workers, however, that we find it all but impossible to define an area separate from our work and reserve it exclusively for our private life. We are so accustomed to taking our work home with us that we hardly notice when the concepts that guide our relations at work seep out of our attaché cases and begin to permeate our dwelling places.

The efficiency expert, with his rock-bound faith that no labor should go undivided, has had his eye on the family for a long time. He has gradually parceled out to the butcher, the baker, the driver education instructor, the sex education instructor—and many, many others—tasks which were once a part of the everyday ongoing life of the family. Since all of these things could be done more efficiently by the expert and the specialist, these functions moved out of the family until it lost all of its character as a producing unit and became almost exclusively a consuming unit. I have recently noticed an increase in the number of families making candles. But this stems from a need for an activity and not a need for candles. Therefore, it is not producing at all, but merely a further form of consuming.

Since the end of production is not the end of work in the home, the division of labor is closely followed by the labor-saving devices. Where we once placed the emphasis on laboring in order to earn and save money, we now invest money in household machines in order to save labor, a rather neat inversion of our puritan heritage. What were once tasks to be performed have been transformed into processes to be tended. The washing machine and clothes dryer, the dishwasher, and the garbage disposal unit can be running through their cycles while the whole family gathers in the living room and labors at nothing more than being together and loving one another. But the dynamics of our situation would not permit this little idyll to take place. The social pressures of war, racial disturbances, drugs, and the crisis in education are pressures acting on the family in such a way as to make its members strangers to one another. After having divided its traditional tasks among the experts and the specialists, the nuclear family suffered the final tragedy of the division of its labor of love, with the children seeking love in the "specialist" peer group of Haight-Ashbury and the parents moving into encounter groups in order to learn how to touch each other.

"Experts urge abolition of marriage" has become a familiar headline in our newspapers. Armed with the latest statistics and moved by statistical compassion, the new abolitionists are declaring that the time has come for the dismantling of that peculiar institution, the family. A Sunday editor can always find material on a conference here or an institute there that has just found that marriage is a pollution problem which could be cleared up if we could only get the right laws passed or repealed. Three-quarter page advertisements for new home furniture are often flanked by columns bearing the latest documentation on the failure of marriage to "meet the needs of modern society." The basic statistics in the indictment are usually the divorce rate: one of every four marriages in the United States; the teen-age subcategory approaches one divorce for every two marriages; and the rate of illegitimacy is 22.5 out of every thousand births.

The workload of the expert is always increasing because he deals in statistics and there is no action or activity that does not tend to become a statistic. Everything becomes information. All of the things we do or are done to us—our births and our deaths, our marriages and our divorces, our vocations and occupations, our very goings and returnings—generate information as inevitably as we produce carbon dioxide by the mere act of exhaling. There is some indication that we are developing the same kind of cycle with the computer that we have always had with the plant life in our natural environment; we generate information and the computer takes this information and transmutes it into strange and wonderful crystals of knowledge. Just as the shaman once mediated between the spirit of the forest and his fellow tribesmen, so the expert is our link with the computer. It is not a closed shop! If you are in possession of a set of statistics and are asked to express your opinion for publication, then chances are that you are an expert.

Experts, whose urgings are calculated to help marriage meet "the needs of modern society," invariably call for a change in the legal status of married couples so that their relationship may be more easily dissolved. This legalistic approach and the motivation behind it can perhaps be shown through a couple of typical examples. A certain psychologist had proposed that marriage become a "nonlegal, voluntary association" between a man and a woman. When asked what might be some of the advantages of taking marriage out of the legal sphere he replied, "First, there would be the elimination of the nonsense about divorce proceedings . . ." Another suggestion, this time by a woman psychiatric worker, is that marriage should be a five-year contract subject to either renewal or cancellation. This would enable the participants to go through an apprentice period to test their compatibility "because such important learning is now denied them in an effort to preserve the fiction of chastity." Any children which were left over after a contract cancellation would be turned over to substitute parents specially trained in child-rearing since "the significance of blood ties is mostly in our heads."

In the light of the suggestions of these apostles of "modern society," the needs of that society begin to emerge with greater clarity. The greatest concern is for compatibility and effortless disengagement. The wish to eliminate "the nonsense about divorce proceedings" may be a good thing in itself but it reveals no concern at all for the quality of the life that must be lived within the relationship of marriage. What possible benefit could married life enjoy from being placed under the terms of a five-year contract? The use of the terms "apprentice" and "compatibility" are revealing, but the complete cynicism of this suggestion is shown in the provision that is made for children whose family contract has run out: turn them over to substitute parents who have been specially trained in the rearing of children. Apparently, in a world in which there is no end to qualified personnel, the most basic demand of human responsibility can be thrown out the window with a cancelled contract. Where will these qualified personnel come from? How will they be trained? Could a society which does not "need" a family based on fidelity really supply substitute parents? Undoubtedly the state would take care of all that. The important thing now is that no responsibility be attached to family relationships.

The true significance of those statistics begins to come through now, also. One divorce for every four marriages fails the needs of modern society not because one marriage failed but because three of them show a needless tendency toward permanence. The fact that out of every thousand births 22.5 are illegitimate represents a small but promising head start toward getting children into the hands of substitute parents.

The point of all this is that "modern society" does not need marriage and the family at all. What it does need is an ever more flexible relationship that may be dissolved at will; a relationship built on the compatibility of personnel and not complicated by any form of commitment. The industrial revolution proved that the family is not necessary to the process of production; now the technological revolution is proving that the family is not necessary to sustaining a high level of consumption.

Because of the troubles in our society we say that our institutions have broken down and failed. Is that really true? Would it not be just as true, and perhaps far more so, to say that our institutions have been spectacularly successful, but that we have been unable to accept the meaning of their success? We have all heard the line, "The operation was a success but the patient died." Which of our institutions has failed? There has never been anything like our productive capacity, and the incentive to consume the fruits of production is so great that the disposal of packaging matter is now a major problem. Our children all begin school and are rapidly caught up in the process of determining who can follow directions and who cannot. Those who exhibit patience and tenacity enough to graduate are then given more important directions to follow than are those who have dropped out. Some of the children fail but the institution of the school does not fail. It operates perfectly as the clearing house that we intend it to be. Has the Church failed? Hardly. Faith is the business of the Church and it has inspired more blind faith in the unexamined workings of our society than anyone could reasonably have asked. Surely no one is going to say that our technological establishment has failed; not with all of those unfading footprints on the moon and with a crew of men taking a Berlitz course in Martian. Despite the fact that we have not won the war in Vietnam, there is little doubt that we could, in the words of a prominent actor-politician, "pave the whole country over, paint parking stripes on it, and be home by Christmas." Any Christmas that we choose.

The family—surely the institution of the family has failed? Not at all. The family has been so successful that it has completed its assigned task well ahead of schedule and is temporarily out of work. Its assignment had been the consumption of goods and services in an expanding economy and with a rising standard of living, and it did this so efficiently that each of its members has learned to consume on its own. The family is now temporarily uninhabited.

The sources of the family of the future are already in our midst, but they are not part of a campaign to change the laws governing marriage and divorce. They are far more interested in a transformation of consciousness than in the clauses of a five-year contract. The community property concerning them most is not what the judge divides up after the divorce, but the world in which we all live, both the natural and the social world. Their most keenly felt need is to find new ways of seeing themselves in action in this world. I am referring to those elements of our youth who, through the life styles they are adopting, are trying to realize ways in which they may live their lives as persons rather than personnel. These young people do not have great respect for ancient institutions, so I am not trying to suggest that they are going about the business of shoring up the foundations of the family. How they might laugh at any such suggestion since so many of them come from what I have called the uninhabited family. Many of them have adopted a style of openness to experience that is not cluttered with inordinate concern for a high standard of living. They are very likely to realize values in their own lives that will lead them to establish families based on the realities of human experience rather than on the drive toward a particular standard of living. The unwillingness to let any institution stand between the person and his experience, the emotional honesty so prominent in the lyrics of rock songs, the lack of sentimentality in the approach to sexuality are attitudes likely to result, in the more stable youth, in a strong and lasting marriage relationship.

The family has a future. Those who are now leaving home are not doing so to escape a family, they are leaving in order to find a family. It is as though they were haunted by the question of Jesus, "Who is my mother, and who are my brothers?" A sense of community is growing from the many forms of group experience, through the rock groups, to the urban and rural communes. It is small, but it is growing. Out of this sense of community there will grow an awareness of the strength and beauty of a marriage free from contract of any length and undertaken in a spirit of fidelity, with a commitment to live face to face. "Here are my mother and my brothers!"

The family lies ahead.

FIDELITY AND FULFILLMENT

8

Janet Golden

When the question of the survival of the family is raised, one suspects that there is some underlying uneasiness that prompted the question, and most often not just a general uneasiness, but one that is quite specific. I am sure that there is more than one cause for apprehension. We may be alarmed, for instance, by the large number of marriages between very young people, with their high incidence of divorce. It may be the breaking up of older, seemingly stable marriages which crumble inexplicably in middle age that particularly trouble us. Or perhaps our alarm springs from a vivid sense of the fragility of so many families in their present-day state of isolation. As Schillebeeckx puts it in his study *Marriage—Human Reality and Saving Mystery:* "One of the consequences of the extremely functionalized character of modern society is that personal problems—sorrow as well as joy—remain within the family circle. It is precisely in these personal elements that society leaves the members of the family alone. That is why there is such need for a comprehensive spiritual 'national health service' to provide spiritual, psychological, psychiatric and other kinds of assistance at all levels for families which, in modern society, have been thrown back on their own resources."

Any of these aspects of modern marriage and indeed many others may unsettle us. Primarily, however, I would like to discuss one rather basic cause for alarm: the sense that women, in re-evaluating their roles in marriage and society, may be abandoning their basic faithfulness to their husbands and to their children. It is indeed a basic anxiety, for if this fidelity should become deeply eroded, what would be the future of the family?

It seems to me that this concern about the stability of the family is being directed particularly at women, because it is sensed that in women's attitudes today, we are dealing with something new. This attitude is newly threatening because what is involved is not the attraction to another person—the perennial sort of infidelity—but the attraction to other values, to a different kind of life altogether than that centered around the family.

What is this unrest among women? It has been stated in a very general way by Dr. Philip Hauser, chairman of the University of Chicago's sociology department, that women are in process of changing "from females to human beings." Such a process inevitably involves problems of identity, and Betty Friedan's thesis that women cannot find their identity through others, her husband and her children, but only in work that uses her full capacities certainly comes to mind. As a specific and militant statement of this redefinition of self, I would like to draw on a letter published in the February 7, 1968, issue of the *National Catholic Reporter*. Its writer, Elaine E. Derso, states that "On a strictly personal level, in three-and-one-half years of marriage, I have met only one priest who is not deeply suspicious of me because 1) I am not yet pregnant; 2) I intend to complete work for the Ph.D. degree, although married; 3) I intend to work all my married life, to cultivate my mind as well as the fruits of my body; and, most controversially, 4) I have rejected that humiliating symbol of female dependency upon the male, my husband's name . . . God gave me my mind, as well as my body—

neither one should be sacrificed to the other. God made both men and women—neither one should be sacrificed to the other."

Although this statement may be taken, at least in Catholic circles as among the more avant of the avant-garde, it is clearly one attempt to work out the transition from female to human being, an attempt that is ordinarily made more tentatively and with less rancor. It would be a mistake, however, to imagine that this rancor represents an isolated instance or even that it is an extreme instance. The writer, after all, *is* married and seems to project future fruits of her body. In other words, she has not quite given up on either husband or children. In both these respects she is an out-and-out traditionalist compared to the members of some of the current Women's Liberation movement. In addition to dumping such minor impedimenta as bras and cosmetics, they would advocate avoidance of marriage, the nuclear family, pregnancy, and, if necessary, sex, which "is not a basic need."

Very likely this relatively small and fragmented movement does not represent the wave of the future. Still in one form or another this groping towards a more complete identity does exist. Even if this search has not in the past seemed to be very pressing during the early crowded years of married life, it has been forced upon many women by the presence of a "second life" that they have been obliged to fill once their children have grown, a second life in which the former definitions of mother and housewife are no longer adequate.

Actually, I would suspect that the option of postponing one's identity crisis to some later stage in life is one that is rapidly eroding. To cite only one reason, one of the more obvious aspects of being female, woman's fertility, and with it, all that was involved with her one-time life work of maternity and childrearing is under increasingly heavy attack. As we enter the seventies, the world is acutely conscious of the threat of overpopulation, and the whole life style of raising a large family of children would seem to be more and more an exceptional choice in the future, even if it does not come to be actually controlled by government.

Possibly this sounds alarmist. But James Reston remarks, in a recent column, that a "big change is taking place in the language of politics. Officials are not only . . . tossing around a new vocabulary of environment, pollution, and ecology, but they are talking about '*control* of the growth of population.'

"They are saying, in short, that the United States will not be able to 'control' pollution of the atmosphere, or the rivers and the seas unless it 'controls' the population of the U.S., and this word control is being used quite consciously now as a substitute for 'family planning.'" In the same column, Mr. Reston quoted President Nixon as saying that fertility "has been the key to the survival of every species. And now for the first time in earth's history, there has emerged one creature for which fertility is not a blessing but a curse. That creature is man . . . Can we reverse the urges of a billion years of evolving life? Can we reverse the cultural traditions of thousands of years of human civilization? We can."

It is kindly of President Nixon to pose this problem as man's, but in point of fact, it is mainly woman's. Not only is there the practical implication that the desired one- or two-child family is going to take up a shrinking fraction of a woman's life, there is the quite unsubtle pressure on the young woman today to redefine herself. If maternity is no longer seen as a value, but on the contrary, poses a threat, how is she to see herself, and in what direction is she to go? She may be further urged to this self-examination by the currently popular suggestion that some form of the Israeli kibbutz would be a more satisfactory way to raise children than the nuclear family with its multiple hang-ups and pressures. Young or middle-aged women—perhaps the old escape—are being forced to see themselves newly. It is the exaggerated examples of this rethinking process, of course, which focus most of the attention and concern about the family and its survival.

As a concern, it is very much akin to that malaise that one feels at the spectacle of so many priests leaving the priesthood, however much one may sympathize with the dilemmas of individual priests. There is a similarity in the urge to redefine oneself and most particularly in the thrust towards greater self-fulfillment, although this fulfillment may seem to be sought in quite opposite directions. For the priest, the direction may be one of deep involvement with another person in marriage and for the woman the freedom to express herself outside the circle of close personal involvement in her family. I say 'seems' because it is really a matter of emphasis. Frequently both the priest and the discontented woman are looking for fulfillment in a combination of meaningful work and personal relationship.

In any case, the malaise evoked is quite similar. We are anxious, and not the least reason for our anxiety is that we feel the ground shaking under our own feet. Every apparent falling away from fidelity can trouble us. If sacred, lifelong promises can be set aside, then where is the permanency in my promises, my state of life? Am I to be obligated more by own projected fulfillment than by any other consideration? Along with this uncertainty goes the quite human anxiety that sooner or later this thrust for fulfillment, even if I should manage to escape it as a personal dilemma, may rebound in a most practical way on me. As a layman I may worry that sooner or later there will not be enough priests to say Mass or hear my confession. A husband may worry that all this unrest will eventually lead to no dinner on the table, and 'latch-key' children. As the Beatles put it most basically: "Will you still need me, will you still feed me, when I'm sixty-four?"

In our anxiety we reiterate rather loudly that the woman *ought* to see that the real source of her fulfillment lies in the family. The priest *ought* to see that the real center of his life is the Mass and the sacraments, that he is giving up something inestimably valuable. And yet, even if these statements are true, they do not solve the problem of people who can no longer feel them to be true. Confidence in fidelity is something that is as important as it is comforting. But there is, in our time, no easy short-cut towards maintaining or regaining it.

Perhaps in the past we have managed to persuade ourselves that we can and should condition people to be faithful, whether to another person or simply to a promise. Women were conditioned by a thousand and one expectations and nudges towards a certain view of themselves and their lives. They were expected to emerge from this conditioning with the conviction that they would find their true happiness and fulfillment in marriage and motherhood, and that they would be foolish to take any other aspect of life very seriously. This, in itself, was some advance over the earlier assumption that marriage, the running of a home, childbearing and rearing were simply the proper business of women and that their happiness and fulfillment were quite irrelevant. As Maurice Chevalier put it, when asked how it felt to be seventy-five: "Wonderful, when you consider the alternative!" (Taking into consideration such evidence as St. Teresa of Avila's rather grim view of what contemporary wives had to put up with, the scepticism about the alternative probably existed on both sides of the convent wall.)

I am not trying to suggest that girls should not learn to cook, or to put it more generally that they should not, if possible, absorb the idea that a happy and faithful marriage is a very splendid "state of life" in which to be. But I do think that the protective attitude that assumes that one knows what is best for the person involved, and can in some way *will* this life for her has been a dangerous one. It was all the more dangerous because it began with the dubious assumption that one knows all about the "nature of woman" and therefore it is perfectly obvious what is best for her.

I say *was dangerous,* not *is dangerous,* because the whole "nature of woman" argument, based as it was on the preeminent importance of uterus and ovaries, is so obviously coming unstuck. Too many people are obviously scared out of their wits by the potentialities of woman's uterus and ovaries for this kind of position to make much headway. In our day most women are going to have to go through the painful experience of finding out for themselves what it does mean to be a woman now, and, most of all, what it means to be this particular woman.

In the process they will have to rediscover the meaning of fidelity in their lives and its relation to the fulfillment they seek. That this process of rediscovery will be painless is probably too much to hope. Right now there are too many women, just as there are too many priests, who feel that they have promised fidelity without knowing what it meant. Some of them will rediscover fidelity as freely chosen by themselves, others will not.

In this rediscovery, it seems to me that one generation will have to try to help the other, or the chances for the future of the family are not terribly bright. It does not seem to me true to say that the young are going to be able to find out all about fidelity for themselves—at least in any great numbers—or that an older generation can tell them everything about it. This may be true of many values, but it is peculiarly true of fidelity because it combines two elements, time and vision, and each generation is likely to know more about one than the other. Fidelity without vision is a habit—sometimes even a bad habit—and fidelity without time is no more than a beginning, the seed of what might be.

The young do not know very much about time because they have not had very much of it. Above all, they have not had the experience of time as a long-term commitment to others as a way of knowing and loving the meaning of another person. Consequently, although there is an enormous amount of talk in the present generation about "meaningful relationships," the meaning is usually confined to what is happening between two people right now. Important as the right now is, it leaves out a lot. As the Ryans put it in their book *Love and Sexuality: A Christian Approach:* "If history is an essential dimension of human personhood as we know it, how can one fully commit himself to another without committing oneself to his on-going history, to what one hopes to aid him to become as well as to what he is?" There is an almost inexpressible joy in seeing a loved person, whether a child or an adult, grow to be more himself, but it is not an instant joy. It takes time.

To put it another way, there are two possible kinds of meaning in a meaningful relationship. There is the meaning that I see in the other person that involves the wonder of discovery and a sort of celebration that this other person exists. The second meaning is how this discovery of the other person makes me feel—alive, joyful, fulfilled, or whatever. How we understand the importance of these meanings makes a great deal of difference, a difference to the individual and a difference to the society in which we live. If we attach the greatest importance to the second part of the meaning, then the tendency is towards the other person becoming replaceable or expendable, because it is the experience and not the person which counts. The obvious and perennial example of this is the person who goes from one love affair or marriage to another. But it could apply also to some aspects of group therapy or dynamics in which a person uses or even manipulates the deep feelings of others in order to feel more alive himself. (This is not to say that a group experience *has* to do this; particularly if it is prolonged, it could lead to an emphasis on the first kind of meaning and a heightened awareness of the wonder and great value of other people. It is simply one of its dangers.)

If we put our emphasis on the first meaning, on the sense of the value and mystery and wonder of the other person, then we are somehow drawn into time and a sense of something that is irreplaceable and inexhaustible. There is a pull to know about this person's past and to be concerned with his future. We may even have the feeling, ridiculous though this seems, that this person is worth a lifetime of loving exploration and commitment. This is the vision in which fidelity is born and needs to be reborn throughout married life.

It is a birth and a beginning, but it does not necessarily follow that there should be an almost instant jump from vision to permanent commitment, and that this is how fidelity develops. All too often one or both may not be mature enough yet for such a commitment, or they may find that they are singularly ill-adapted to help each other grow in love. Before children are added to the commitment, some kind of testing ground for fidelity more adequate than the conventional rather brief engagement may be indicated.

Some of the more thoughtful young have revolted against the idea that marriage is a sort of initiation rite into adulthood, that you marry in order to grow up. One of them, Mark Gerzon, in *The Whole World Is Watching,* states that the "postwar generation has concluded that if the divorce rate is not to continue to rise, deep premarital relationships will have to become acceptable. This generation's solution has been, thanks to the pill, for two people to try to know each other deeply and intimately, to establish a long-standing loyalty to each other by living and making love together, and then, when they knew each other as adults, to get married. This is neither immoral nor harmful nor loose. It is simply an attempt to avoid divorce and to assure their children of a loving, two-parent home—the kind of home which an unprecedented number in this generation have gone without."

Obviously this kind of relationship is not the only possible answer, or for that matter the best answer. There is, for instance Father Evely's suggestion, in *Lovers in Marriage,* that there should be a long and intensive period of exploration and preparation for marriage, lasting about three years, preferably without premarital sexual relations. He has also suggested that the Church should establish a novitiate for marriage, a period of two or three years during which a couple would live in a civil marriage without having children and would receive some kind of guidance in forming a home.

It is my own feeling that this kind of provisional fidelity or apprenticeship to fidelity presents women with special opportunities and difficulties. All of them, in one way or another, provide the opportunity for a woman to develop the relationship between herself and the man she has chosen which is too often short-circuited by the pattern of early childbearing and rearing. Too many women become mothers before they have ever learned to be wives, and once the relationship between the two is out of balance it can be very difficult to put right again, difficult perhaps even to see. Motherhood can be the evasion of the risks and difficulties of a fully adult relationship. The sort of fidelity, "for the sake of the children," that develops out of this sort of unbalanced motherhood is likely to collapse when the children have grown, and is cruelly unfair to the children themselves. All this, any sort of prolonged trial period without children would be likely to circumvent.

Another positive aspect of such a trial period is that it would give a young woman time to develop further whatever interests or abilities she has outside the home, or if she does not have them, endeavor to discover them. Obviously this is an opportunity rather than a certain outcome. She can spend the time she would otherwise be spending on her children in going out and getting a routine job that fails to develop her in any way; or she can sit home and polish the furniture and look at soap operas. But the very fact that she is trying to develop an adult, one-to-one relationship with another person might force her in the direction of trying to be more of a person herself. This might mean studying. It might mean work, volunteer or paid, full or part-time. Whatever the practicalities might be, it could be leading her towards a sort of sturdiness and liberty of spirit in which she would neither expect a husband to provide her with a happiness and interest in life that she was unable to find for herself, nor children to give her a reason for her existence.

The difficulty that I can see in this kind of period lies precisely in the somewhat ambiguous quality of the fidelity that it demands. Of the three possibilities mentioned, the long engagement, living together in a sort of trial marriage, or the civil marriage as novitiate to the sacramental marriage, the engagement clearly presents the least difficulty of this kind. By its nature it calls for a provisional fidelity. It is a testing and a limited kind of testing, trying to estimate the probabilities for success of a full commitment, but not claiming to test the commitment itself. Living in a trial situation which both is and is not a full marriage is quite different. To this member of an older generation it seems to have a sort of built-in shakiness that is alarming. Learning to live together can be difficult enough, without adding the notion that one is somehow taken home on approval like a slightly doubtful dress from a department store. Admittedly, this may not be the way that the people concerned really see it. What they mistrust may not be the other person but the institution of marriage as they know it, and their commitment to each other may be unshakeable. But if it is not, then it seems to me that the absence of a genuine fidelity makes a very poor seed ground for the sort of personal growth that the two people are looking for.

I spoke of fidelity as containing two elements, vision and time, but the third element linking the two is commitment, the commitment to work out, in time, one's vision of the great value and lovableness of the other person, and to keep working at it even when the vision gets very blurry indeed. In effect, fidelity says to the partner in marriage, and later to each child, "I believe in you and I will not give up on you."

Without this assurance, anything and everything can be a mortal threat to the relationship, a fight, temporary boredom, a spreading waistline, a misunderstanding, or an unshared interest. Fidelity does not mean greeting any and every kind of behavior in one's partner with applause or resignation, but it does mean enough faith in the shared life with this other person to allow him or her growing room, living room, room to make mistakes, take risks, and have bad moments. Obviously, what I am saying applies with at least equal force to sexual relations, where an atmosphere of being on trial would hardly be the most helpful.

It would be a great misfortune if a large number of this generation believed that fidelity in a relationship meant the opposite of freedom, and that the way to really love another person was without asking for or giving commitment. On the contrary, it seems to me that the essential freedom to be and grow to be oneself is built on the foundation of fidelity given and received. However, unless one takes an unduly grim view of human nature, one suspects that this is something that some people of any generation who really love each other will tend to discover.

All this may seem to be wandering rather far afield from the specific problem of women's fidelity or lack of it in re-evaluating their roles in marriage and society. In actuality, I think it is very much to the point. If this kind of relationship of valuing and belief and commitment grows up between two people, which I have tried to suggest is a relationship of fidelity, then the problems of working out family life in a rapidly changing society become manageable and unthreatening. If a man gives his fidelity to this particular woman with all her various capacities and potentialities and not to a sort of collection of roles—housekeeper, sex partner, child-tender, hostess, or what have you—then he is certainly not going to feel threatened by infidelity by whatever in her does not fit into these boxes. On the contrary, if being a poet or a political organizer or a scientist is part of this person he loves and values, he is going to want to see that part of her kept alive, perhaps even more at some time than she. He would wish to see her develop herself to the fullest extent of which she is capable over the course of her lifetime, just as she would wish the same for him.

It seems to me very unlikely that women who are secure in this kind of fidelity and give it in return are going to be irresponsible about the needs of their families. Being valued as a person makes it more possible to see and respond to the values in other persons, husband and children who make up the family. Hopefully, such women would have the balance to avoid using their children whether in a large family or a small as extensions of themselves or keys to their own miserably precarious sense of fulfillment. They could cope then more realistically with the projected small family of the future, because they would have a sense of self that extended beyond motherhood, and that would not require of them to concentrate the time and attention on two children that would have been appropriately spread out among six. (Or they might, in some cases, quite reasonably judge that the best of their abilities were brought out in childraising and decide to adopt a large family.) On the other hand, caring and being cared for, they would not be inclined to jeopardize the upbringing of their children by pulling out when they were needed in order to take a job as another kind of proof of themselves, or instant fulfillment.

I am rather hesitant to talk about fulfillment in connection with the family because I think of it as a somewhat chancy word and a seldom more than very imperfect reality. For most people one would suppose that fulfillment would represent a combination of personal relationships that met their need to give and receive love and work that used a reasonable amount of their capacities, presumably work which was in some sense creative. By this definition, there are probably very few fulfilled people in our society, men or women. If anything, I would suspect that the majority of women may have a slight edge, at least for part of their lives, because they get more satisfaction out of their families than their husbands do out of their largely meaningless jobs.

Because fulfillment does combine both of these aspects, although in a different balance of one over the other for different people, it would seem to me as much of a mistake to expect marriage and family relationships to solve all the problems of fulfillment as it is to look for it in outside achievement. The sort of privatism, for instance, which sees almost all outside interests, relationships and commitments as a potential threat to the married relationship seems to me very dangerous. I do not really believe in a "we two against the world" attitude.

On the other hand, if the family is not thought of as a self-enclosed answer to fulfillment, but as a place where people, husband

and wife and children may be mutually supported in growing towards fulfillment, it may be in a sense the best answer we have. Admittedly it is an imperfect answer with its full share of frustrations and conflicting demands. But if one believes that fidelity as a bond of belief and commitment fosters personal growth, then one may hope that the family can and will survive.

A NEW KIND OF FAMILY?

9

Rosemary Haughton

There is a certain very widespread climate of thought in which any ideas connected with "the family" sound distinctly stuffy. The very word "family" has a restrictive, respectable, nineteenth-century-comfortable-middle-class atmosphere about it. The reaction against a version of family life that was indeed very restrictive has produced a state of affairs in which people who value freedom, independence, personal integrity and maturity—all the "in" things—regard family life, as such, as almost inevitably a restriction on their desires. So people talk about free love, easy divorce, the example of the "kibbutzim" in Israel as a method of childrearing that frees women, especially, from domesticity. Love should be spontaneous, not controlled by deadening law, and so on. So the prophets predict the end of "the family" and speculate about what comes next. Polygamy? Baby farms? Selective breeding, *à la* Plato, with communal nurseries?

The Christian reaction to this kind of thing is usually a defensive one. It is very familiar. "Uphold the values of family life" (which means a patriarchal-type family with the moral notions of the nineteenth century at its stuffiest); "The family that prays together, stays together" (and one is not expected to wonder why staying together is so desirable for Christians with a world mission). The methods advocated for preserving "the Christian family" are daily rosary, emphasis on parental discipline, careful censorship of books, and the impossibility of divorce for Catholics, so that those who do divorce automatically cease to be Catholics, and in so doing, preserve the standard of Catholic fidelity and permanence in marriage.

This situation, which would otherwise be reasonably clear-cut (faithful families on one side, worldly nonfamilies on the other) is complicated by two things. One is that the traditional Catholic family *at its best* is quite clearly a marvelous achievement, a community of hope and love and enterprising, flexible energy. The other is that Catholic couples who are devoted to each other and to their children are often among those who are most uncomfortable with the traditional "Catholic family" ideal. They want to *be* a family, yet they realize all the force of the criticisms leveled at the family as a stereotype. They are often both fervent Christians and fervently modern in their social and ethical outlook, and this places them in a painful dilemma to which they see no resolution.

What I would like to do here is not to try to solve all the problems (which no one can do anyway), but to help people to begin solving them by showing, first of all, in which way the *problem* is misconceived and misstated. Secondly, I want to suggest how the proper stating of the problem indicates a way in which it might be solved.

It seems to me there is a basic confusion here that is not normally noticed. It stems from the fact that Christianity grew up in a certain cultural milieu, and therefore necessarily expressed itself in terms of that culture. People in Europe in the Middle Ages were Christian, and they were medieval Europeans, whose way of life was shaped by all kinds of odd circumstances that had nothing whatever to do with their religion. But they *were* Christians, and they lived that way *as* Christians, even if only nominally. So it was natural to assume that this was the ethics and all. It became accepted as, simply, Catholic Christianity, traditional and normal. Of course, it did change as time passed, but the changes were not really noticed as such, so that nineteenth-century Catholics could feel they were *the same kind of people* as medieval Catholics and regard their Catholic culture (which was in fact widely different) as the traditional one. This meant that their whole notion of family life seemed to them traditional and Catholic. Any other kind of family life was *not* traditional, and therefore not properly Catholic.

It is possible now, with our historical hindsight, to see how this happened. We also have access to many more studies by anthropologists and sociologists of cultures totally different from ours; and in which patterns of sexual behavior and family living are quite different, too. Although it may be difficult to make such a leap of imagination, it is possible to realize that there might be Christian couples, and family arrangements of Christians, that are widely different from our own, and yet these people would still be Christians. So we can calm down and realize that if strange things happen to the patterns of marriage and family life in our own society this does not necessarily make it impossible for Christians to live their faith, as married, and as a family.

We can now go on, therefore, to distinguish between the notion of family life that Christians have happened to accept and live in the West, until recently, and the notion of "the Christian family" which is a very different thing and could be embodied in a number of different sociological patterns of relationships. The pattern of family life to which we are accustomed is only one possible one among many. As such, it is no more Christian than any other. What makes it Christian is the quality of Christian living that goes on in the family grouping, not the sexual and familial conventions of the particular society.

Here we have to make a very important reservation. I said that a changed pattern of family life—even one we would scarcely recognize as a family in our traditional sense—would not necessarily make it impossible for Christians to live their faith in it, and that Christian living could be embodied in a number of different patterns of which ours is only one, in itself no more Christian than any others. If other forms of family life are not necessarily unsuitable vehicles for Christian living they nevertheless *can* be unsuitable. There may be patterns of family life that make it virtually impossible for Christians to embody their faith without breaking out of that pattern. There may be others in which Christian living is not impossible but muted and ineffective. And there may be some which can be a proper framework for Christian living. What none of them can be is actually Christian, in the sense that this way of living, as such, is an expression of Christian faith. Being a Christian is something that happens to people, because they have faith and their faith demands certain things of them. The customs and conventions of their culture are the setting for that faith. They can never take its place.

It may be interesting to take a few examples of differing types of family patterns, just to see how varied these can be, and still be a family of some kind. The Trobriand Islanders, studied by Malinowski, had a matrilineal type of society, in which the father had little influence in the children's lives. The male authority in the family was the mother's brother. It was he who excited the various kinds of authority-tensions, the jealousies and rebellions, that we tend to associate with the father's position in the family. He arranged the marriages of the girls, and since the property descended through the girls this was important. Weaning was late and unhurried, so that many of the emotional tensions often associated with mother-child relationships in our society were absent; the relationship was, in fact, relaxed and not especially close. But a boy's whole life— social and economic—depended upon this relationship. He might have to support his mother, and her home remained his second home. His father might become a companion and friend, but had no authority over him. (In such a society, God might have been named as "Uncle" rather than "Father." Our shock at this idea shows how set are our ideas of family.) Boys and girls of all ages played together freely and without much supervision, and play included sex-play, right into adolescence. At this stage boys moved out of the home into special houses for unmarried men, where the girls joined them at night if they wished. The only exception to this sexual permissiveness was the brother-sister relationship. Brother and sister were taught to keep apart from an early age, and not even to speak to each other. The one absolutely forbidden and horrifying sin was brother-sister incest. Other forms of incest, while not approved, did not carry this stigma.

The Manus of New Guinea, studied by Margaret Mead, were highly puritanical and materialistic in outlook, their religion being mostly a set of superstitions connected with ghosts of the dead. Sex was regarded as disgusting, and women dreaded it and found no satisfaction in it. Relationships between parents and young children, however, were close and warm and very permissive, so that sub-adolescent children had almost complete freedom. After that, adult repressions and taboos clamped down. Unlike the Trobrianders, however, the Manus allowed a good deal of sex-play, short of inter-course, between cousins even after both were married, and close friendships between brother and sister. This compensated to some extent for lack of any sex-play or tenderness in marriage, in which intercourse was brief, without tenderness or fun, and of course without foreplay. Marriages were arranged on a strictly financial basis and "love" was therefore discouraged in every possible way.

There is a vague, wistful sort of myth current among many ad-vocates of sexual permissiveness in our own society, to the effect that Polynesians live (or lived) in an earthly paradise where lack of sexual guilt sets them free from repressions, where aggression does not exist and everyone is happy. A rather closer look presents a different picture. There certainly is a great degree of sexual permis-siveness in most of the islands, at least among the lower classes of society. Girls of high birth, however, are closely guarded since their virginity is necessary to their prestige or marriage. In one tribe such a girl, when a marriage has been arranged, must have her hymen broken in public by the chief, who must hold up bloodied fingers to prove her virginity. She is then paraded, naked and still bleeding, before the guests to demonstrate the fact to everyone's satisfaction. If by any chance there is no bleeding, the unfortunate girl is clubbed to death on the spot by her outraged relatives. This exclusiveness among the high-born, however, is not due to any notion of sexual restraint or purity, but is related to the virgin's social value. There is not much of what we would call love involved in sex in any case. A chief's wife who finds her husband too demanding may recommend him to add another wife or two, but most men are monogamous, in a sense, though the wife's sister (or two) are extra bed-fellows for him and no one worries too much about any other adventures he may have. There is no limit whatever to premarital sex among the lower classes. It is the most usual amusement, even among small children, as far as they can. Children are treated with tolerance and affection and have several alternative "mothers," so that intense mother-child emotions are unlikely. These people are (or were) notably light-hearted and easy-going, and it was understandable that this should be interpreted by repressed Westerners as an expression of almost paradisal innocence and goodness before guilt clouded the picture. This notion of the noble savage is somewhat modified by the discovery that the unwanted babies, who were inevitably numerous in a society where sex is everybody's game and there is no contraception, used to be killed off with the same relaxed, cheerful matter-of-factness with which they were conceived. The mothers often did it themselves. One woman, asked how many babies she had disposed of, replied casually, "Seventeen." Marriages are easily dissolved, so no one worries about marital friction. Perhaps because there is no worry about permanence, unions are, in fact, often lifelong and content.

If we move further off in time rather than space we can take a look at courtly love in the Middle Ages. Marriages were generally arranged according to financial, political, or dynastic needs. Love in marriage was not expected but regarded by some sticklers as a social solecism, according to the rule of chivalry. A knight had his "lady"—though he might well be married—whom he more or less worshipped, served with minute fidelity, and probably never caressed in any manner more intimate than a chaste kiss on the cheek. Frustrated passion was the "in" thing. It was thought to be ennobling. Highborn boys were sent off to another noble household at the age of about seven, to serve strenuously as pages and later as esquires to their lord before they themselves were knighted, looked around for a "lady" and incidentally got married and produced more knightlets, whom they never got to know at all well. Girls were sometimes brought up at home, but often, like their brothers, went to another household and learned domestic arts, most importantly how to sing and dance, the arts of courtesy and the rules of the game of chivalry. Children of low birth had a better time, in some ways, because they stayed with their parents, had time to play (if they were lucky) and could marry whom they liked, at least sometimes. Families might be split up, beggared, or rendered fatherless at the lord's whim. Girls of the peasantry were fair game to the knights who were too chaste to touch their ladies, but did not consider that peasant flesh defiled their knightly honor.

Shift along in time and take a look at upper-class family life in England, only a generation ago. Parents might marry for "love," but if "love" did not last long they need not worry too much because either they belonged in the cosmopolitan world where adultery was normal, provided it was discreet, or they were in the "county" and "polite" society where sex was not quite "nice" (but okay with housemaids or chorus girls, who were not "nice" anyway) and politics, hunting, or making money were acceptable distractions from marital infelicity (or perhaps a-felicity would describe it better). Wives could hunt, too, or sit on committees, or entertain, or enjoy ill health. Children were consigned to nannies—who could be wonderful—and then to nursery governesses, until they went to school. The boys went to prep school at seven, were beaten for the good of their souls, learned not to cry, to distrust girls, to decline Latin nouns, play rugger, and later to get their own back on life by bullying the younger ones. Girls went to school later and played hockey. Sex came into their lives late and undercover. Many girls left school with only the haziest notion of sex, having wept with horror when menstrual periods caught them unawares. Boys in their teens were deeply embarrassed by visits of female relatives, especially mothers, to their schools and, of course, never kissed them. Their early experiments with sex were usually either with other boys, or—a bit later—with servant girls. Relations between children and parents were often tolerantly friendly, sometimes resentful, never close. Aunts and uncles abounded and grandparents could sometimes be closer and more intimate than parents. But Nanny was, in many upper-class homes, the real emotional center of life, everyone's confidant, health of the sick deb, refuge of society sinners, comforter of the afflicted schoolboy, help of, well, even Christians, if any managed to emerge in such an environment.

The point of this brief catalogue of some familial extravaganzas is to put our own worries in perspective. It may be that family life in our society will alter rapidly and radically. We may live to see a sexually permissive society in which divorce is simple and fault-free, and arrangements are made for the children in a practical and uncontentious spirit. Marriage may be rather a common sense, friendly convenience for the sake of the children's stability than an attempt to establish a sexually exclusive and loving relationship. Or we may try bringing up the children in groups, on the pattern of the kibbutz. (If we do this, we had better pay attention to more recent reports of emotional after-effects in children brought up this way.) Compared with some of the pictures of family life which I sketched above, this does not sound so outrageous after all. It certainly is not what we are used to. In that case, what are Christians to do?

Christians are in the world, but not of it. Though they must be fully involved with others, they have a vision of the good of human life, the eternal life of the resurrection, which makes them different. They know that the way there is *love,* of God in man, of man for God's sake, which is his own sake. They must, therefore, *judge* the world, as Christ said. They judge the world, and that means its family structures, its sexual ethics, and customs, by this standard of the risen life. We have to ask, do these ways of living our married and family life make it possible for people to respond to Christ? Can they really *love* in such a setting? In so far as they *can,* this is, then, an acceptable setting for Christian living, even if it is unfamiliar. Insofar as it prevents love, or distorts it or dissipates it or degrades it, then this is *not* a possible way of life for those who are Christ's, nor can they bear witness to him in such a setting. They can only oppose it and live in opposition to it, even if that means social (or even actual) martyrdom.

Although the way family patterns are changing in our society may at first sight seem to be leading us into an anti-Christian structure, it may not be so. What we are likely to have (have already, to some extent) is a more open and flexible family pattern. Easy divorce does not mean people *have* to divorce. It could mean that the value of Christian love and fidelity in marriage would be all the more apparent, because not imposed by convention but only by real love, hope and faith. Mobility of children need not mean rootless teen-agers, it could mean that children of Christians could grow up confident in their parents' love, but aware, also, that all the world is peopled with their brothers and sisters whom they and their parents can welcome and serve and love.

Finally there is one more kind of family pattern we can look to, that may help to know what I mean and give us a concrete example from which to start as we try to make families of the future really Christian.

This kind of family lives in a world that is rapidly changing, in which efficient transport makes for mobility and trade, and cultural exchange leads to mixtures of races and cultures. It is a world more or less at peace, except for rebellions in areas that seem, to most people, fairly remote. It is a world full of different and rival religions and of philosophies aiming to displace religion, in which government pays lip-service to official religion but ignores its values in practice and, at least theoretically, treats all creeds and races alike. It is a world of class privilege, and of racial privilege, most unacknowledged but quite real; of wide division between rich and poor. It is also a world whose traditional pattern is visibly beginning to break up, so that the young, and other unstable elements, are a worry to politicians; interest in the occult, in eroticism, and in mysticism are great, as always at such periods.

It seems very familiar. In fact, it is the world in which the Gospel was first preached, the Roman world of the first century. In it we can see three main types of family life, which are again curiously familiar. That of the rich is still much what it was before the crack-up began. Couples are protected from friction in marriages made for money or prestige by the separateness of their lives. Wives are for breeding. Amusement is sought among more enterprising females. Wives, more quietly, can get their bit of fun on the side, also. Children are brought up by servants, boys are taught to despise women, and so on. The families of the very poor have little chance to form a pattern at all. The labor market and the wishes of employers, sheer necessity or the police, push them around, separate wives from husbands and children from parents. A "home" is something unknown. They live somewhere, if they can, but someone else decides where, and for how long and under what conditions. Family affection is a furtively snatched privilege that has no security, no future. For slaves, there is no marriage, no family life at all. The young from poor families—boys or girls—are there for the use of the rich and of anyone else who has a bit of money. (We have no slaves now, or so we say, but this description fits the poor of our big cities uncomfortably well. Nowadays, as then, the poor are always wrong.)

The third kind of family is that of the shopkeepers, the artisans and craftsmen, the clerks and teachers, the small merchants and some people with little businesses, a reasonable independence, in other words, the much maligned middle class. We think of middle-class families as keeping themselves to themselves, enclosed in protective isolation, respectable and prudish. These people were not. They were too exposed for that, exposed to ideas, to the moving populations, to the vagaries of the market, to the brutality of the upper class and of the police, unless they had a rich friend. Parents often stayed together, if only because they were part of an economic unit: the wife helped. Unfaithfulness was normal, though. Children grew up early and had to learn a trade or craft. They married young and might move a long way off or stay on in the same house. Teen-agers had little supervision—no one had time—and had to work things out for themselves. But there was much mutual affection and support; a lot of coming and going of friends and neighbors in the home.

The first Christian converts were mostly of this kind, though there were many among the slaves and the poor and even a few rich and noble. In *each* case Christian faith demanded to be embodied in daily living. For the rich, the traditional pattern would not do. It contradicted too much of the new faith. Either the faith or the family pattern had to give way, and we can see in Paul's letter to Philemon a case where the family pattern did give. The returning slave is welcomed as "a dear brother," an unheard-of notion.

To the degraded and harried families of the poor the new faith brought hope and dignity. It *created* the beginnings of a pattern by its emphasis on the dignity, even for the poor, of married life, a dignity that was a cliché to the respectable, but an outrageous novelty to the poor, and a challenge, nowadays also, to the sincerity of

Christians who expect cleanliness, fidelity, and good manners from people living in subhuman conditions.

For rich and poor the existing way of life was altered by faith, because faith could not survive unless life did alter. In the third case, that of the middle class, the way of life was not basically altered, rather it was transfigured by faith. Unfaithfulness and the prostitution of children and adolescents were forbidden, as well as drunkenness and other unruly behavior, but the way of life, as such, did not need to alter. Its virtues were enhanced and cultivated, its vices gradually pruned away, but the pattern remained. These modest households were normally hospitable, now they opened their hearts to all "the household of the faith." Paul naturally stayed in such households, as did the other apostles and travelling preachers. The poor were welcomed, the sick cared for, the sad comforted.

These homes also became centers of Christian teaching—would-be converts were sent there to learn about their new faith. And the bigger ones were liturgical centers, too, the only "churches" there were. The richer members were naturally able to be more lavish in hospitality and charity, lavish, that is, in welcoming more people, for their standard of life was simple even to sparseness. They were not all saints. The old vices remained. Paul had to rebuke his converts for frequent lapses into pagan behavior, rowdiness or arrogance. They had their values right and they embodied these in a form of family life that was, at least potentially, warm, supporting, comforting (as it must be if love is to begin to grow) but *open*— open to God and to man. Paul classes the practice of hospitality with being "on fire with the Spirit," as qualities he wants to find in his converts. He evidently saw both in his favorite households.

Perhaps we could begin our search for the new form for Christian family life—a form that *can* embody faith—by thinking of it as a "household" rather than a family in the sense simply of a group of blood relations. In some grouping or other, married couples and children will need each other, in order to learn to love and to give; but radiating out from that center of love in marriage, we may have all manner of people who need or appreciate this love and whom the family can include in its circle of service and love.

Our houses are smaller, but our "household," in Paul's sense, need not be. It is a bond of love, not of bricks or timber, that binds such a family. Perhaps we *can* build larger, and share families, spread the burden of work and child care, let children learn to include, not exclude, their fellows by seeing how "these Christians love one another."

It will be hard work to create a truly Christian, loving way of family life in the new society. It was probably even harder for the first Christians. A good way to start thinking about our own problem would be to read the Epistles from this point of view. Allow them to build up an image of a new sort of Christian family, witnessing to the Resurrection in a sick society that desperately needs faith, hope, and love.

THE FUTURES OF THE FAMILY

10

Sally and Philip Scharper

There are, in our day, a goodly number of savants and sophisticated savages who have pronounced the family dead and have gathered, many of them joyfully, for the obsequies.

The family is, of course, neither dead nor dying. It is evolving, as is almost every other arena of human effort, but it is no more dead than the God whose life in Tri-unity represents both the source and goal of that community which is the family.

In this essay, we shall attempt to deal—in admittedly sweeping strokes—with some features of the Christian families of the future. Let us choose a future soon to be upon us, the roots of which are starkly visible in our present. We shall be attempting to discern, therefore, what the Christian family may in part look like and be like in the year 2000, scarcely a generation away.

The first element that will affect the future family is a growing realization that the population explosion is real, is here and by 2000 will have reached near-disaster proportions.

The rapid rise in population in the United States is obviously related to our current ecological crisis. The more people we have, more of our irreplaceable natural resources will be spent, more greenland and woodland will be bulldozed for housing, our mountains of solid waste will grow higher, air and water pollution will outstrip even the crash programs designed to curb them, and the quality of life will decline for all our citizens.

The situation was set forth in dispassionate scientific terms by Dr. Roger Egeberg, Surgeon-General of the United States: ". . . What does freedom of choice in family planning imply in the present state of society? It implies enormous population growth for the simple reason that the typical American family, if it can, will elect to have three children, not two. Thus family planning, in the present state of things, will lead to intractable population growth—to three hundred million Americans by the year 2000."

The ecological crisis has been like the fire bell sounding in a tiny village: almost all of the citizens respond. Political conservatives and liberals, activists and the usually apathetic find themselves side by side in the bucket brigade and manning the fire hoses. Man—modern, technological man—has ravaged nature and befouled his environment to a point where human life as we have known it seems threatened. The realization of this ecological crisis has served to unite the disparate components of our society more than has any cause since World War II.

Most significantly, perhaps, the young have adopted the cause, not least, perhaps, because they have a greater stake in our threatened future than do their elders. College students are demanding courses in ecology, even though the number of qualified teachers for such studies is not much greater than the number equipped to teach black studies. At "environmental teach-ins," they ritually bury an internal combustion engine. They then drive away from the funeral site in their cars and motorcycles, of course; but one cannot demand greater consistency from the young than one expects from their parents.

It is the young who, in all probability, will see more clearly than most the interrelation between the environmental crisis and the population problem. If a doubling of the world's population by 2000 will ravage even more of our already plundered planet, many young parents will choose to have "the two—or preferably one—offspring" that Dr. Egeberg thinks necessary. Some, indeed, may make the extremely heroic decision to have no children at all, becoming "eunuchs for the sake of the Kingdom," understood as the building of the earth into a fit dwelling place for that sacred creature made in the image of God.

The Church will eventually realize that there is a theological dimension to ecology, and will revive its ancient, but long-forgotten understanding that man is not the master of creation, but steward over it. The ruthless exploitation of the earth and ocean (which usually involves the exploitation of other human beings) will be seen as sinful, since it violates man's primal mandate to enter into creative partnership with nature.

From this theological position the Church will move next to the realization that she is the guardian of the quality of life—a role the Church had assumed in its sponsoring of schools, its preservation of the classics of antiquity, its protection of serf and peasant, its elevation of woman (despite the myopia of some of her great theologians), her efforts to impose peace or at least "humanize" the conduct of warfare.

In the context of the ecological crisis the Church might well exhort the married to limit the number of their children to one or two, a sacrifice to be made in the interests of "the greater good," a concept that has long been a hinge-concept in scholastic philosophy and Catholic moral theology.

For those capable of "a yet more excellent way," the Church may recommend having no children, for theological reasons not too dissimilar from those long advanced to support priestly celibacy and the religious vow of chastity.

We may, then, in the foreseeable future see one of those ironies with which "God is so prodigal," in the words of Paul Claudel. The Church, within a generation, may be suggesting through press and pulpit that those couples who refuse to limit their families are guilty of selfishness—a charge leveled by the Church for years against those who did limit their families through means of artificial contraception.

To speak of the Christian family in the year 2000 is immediately to remind ourselves that we are speaking, on the world stage, of people who will be reduced to bit parts and even walk-ons. We are witnessing, even in our own time and even in our own country, the sunset of the white Christian Atlantic community which has dominated world history for the past five millenia. By 2000 that domination will have long been ended.

The new world now at its dawning will be a world, numerically at least, brown, yellow and black—Afro-Asian, secularized and poor. According to some projections, the population of China alone, in the year 2000, may reach 1,700,000,000 people—more than the present population of North and South America, Europe, Russia, and Africa combined.

This world, already in the process of becoming, will also be a global village, as we have often been reminded. A village not only in the sense of almost instant communication, as Marshall McLuhan has pointed out, but a village in the even more radical sense of economic interdependence, wherein a rice famine in China may perhaps threaten starvation in the United States, even as, in 1968, the lives of thousands in India depended on shipments of surplus wheat from the breadbasket plains of North America.

In such a world, those families which are Christian will form a statistically small group, culturally homogeneous perhaps, but not culturally decisive so far as marriage *mores* and expectations are concerned. Indeed, it might not be extreme to say that in the year 2000 the Christian family within the global village may be analogous to the Chinese family within present-day San Francisco.

If we attempt to discern what the basic quality of marriage will be in the diaspora Church of 2000, a reasonable surmise might be that Christians will enter marriage because they will have felt that they were called to it. There will be a more widespread understanding of the *vocation* of Christian marriage in 2000, than in 1971.

The reasons for this are not difficult to see. With so many cultural forces operating against religious faith, to lead a life rooted in supernatural values will represent a decisive choice between belief and nonbelief.

In a world where the major religions will each be known at least as a value system, the Christian will at some point in his life have chosen to be a Christian, in somewhat the same way that young Polish Catholics today must *choose* to be Catholics, since Communism is not only a competing value system, but the one which holds out the added appeals of state support and public privilege.

Christianity, in the global village, will, in all likelihood, be shorn of all the cultural supports which have marked its history from the time of Constantine to our own. To be a Christian will mean to have chosen to be a Christian, rather than to be a Christian because one's family was, or because one's nation had some lingering, almost nostalgic, claim to be a Christian country. "Milieu Christianity" will be dead.

The Christian, under these circumstances, will have a heightened sense of Christian values; he will, therefore, have a clearer understanding of sacramental marriage than was possible to his predecessors in the faith from the time of Christ to the Space Age.

There will have been, first of all, the clarification of marriage that took place within the Church between 1960 and 1980. The failure of Pope Paul VI and his successor to make a binding pronouncement on the morality of means aimed at conception control was seen, after 1975, to have been an exercise of restraint, the magisterium waiting fully to ascertain the *sensus fidelium* in matters pertaining to moral as well as to dogmatic teaching. Whatever the motives of the two Pontiffs may have been, the effects of their nonaction served to show that the people within the Church accepted and adopted what the "world" had accepted long before: that two people entering marriage could choose, as equally moral options, a vocation to either procreative love or to creative love within the context of Christian marriage.

There was a period, in the early '70's, when these terms had occasioned sharp and often bitter discussion. After forests had been turned into woodpulp to bear the conflicting views of *America, Civilta Cattolica, Commonweal, Stimmen der Zeit, Information Cath-*

olique, and *Razon y Fe,* the understanding became clear that reality had once more raced ahead of theory. The restoration of the married deaconate had shown, particularly in those pressure points once called "mission countries," that the majority of such marriages were, in fact, childless, and were childless by choice.

Numerous surveys of this situation were, of course, made by the Meta-sociological Research Institute, established by the Vatican in 1972; the results of the survey showed clearly that the majority of deacons and their wives felt a vocation toward: a) a mutual commitment through sexual expression toward the personal growth of the marriage partner, b) the commitment to shared service of the broader community wherein husband and wife together carried out the Church's mission of reconciliation in the world, and c) the conviction that their shared service of the Word to the world could, in most cases, be more effectively carried out if the apostolic team of husband and wife were free of the responsibilities of parenthood.

Such a development on the existential level helped toward a deeper understanding of marriage on the theological level; the Church now realized and proclaimed that a man and woman could have a vocation to marriage without also having a vocation to parenthood.

Advances in biochemical technology had made it possible to separate sexuality from procreation; theologians saw increasingly that, since parenthood now rested completely on human choice, the choice of parenthood, for the Christian in a densely populated world, should be seen as a married couple's conviction that they had been divinely summoned to be parents. Parenthood came to be seen, in the context of Christian marriage, as a charism, a response to the vocation of procreative love, which demanded psychological maturity and the talents of educator and economist as well.

Those Christian couples who did not feel called to procreative love saw their vocation as one of creative love: their two-in-oneness through indwelling of the Triune God was to be a special sign of God's Presence in and love for the human community, in much the same way as priestly celibacy had been seen as such a special sign for centuries.

When enforced priestly celibacy was abrogated by the Third Vatican Council in 1975, it was largely because the Christian world had come to realize that the sign-value of priestly celibacy as creative love and service to the community was now being more effectively realized through the husband and wife who had sacrificed parenthood in order better to serve the needs of the larger community, particularly through their efforts to restructure world society in the light of justice and human dignity.

Once priesthood was separated from celibacy in the Western Latin Church, the positive relation of priesthood to marriage became more deeply realized. The Christians, a constantly shrinking minority in a civilization which rejected most of their values, found themselves in a situation closely resembling that of the Jews in the diaspora over the past two centuries. Indeed, in certain important respects, the response of the Christian in diaspora was much like that of the Jewish people.

Except for those places on the globe where there were large clusters of Christians, there were few large churches. For the most part, the Christians assembled for the Sunday liturgy and fellowship in small, geodesic structures atop their dwelling complexes or their neighborhood shopping centers. These special liturgies were presided over by priests who served as teachers and counselors for the small group of Christians under their charge.

These priests were usually celibate, and their choice of celibacy as a response to the Spirit was a sign highly valued even beyond the Christian community. The "erotic explosion" of the late '60's had taken a heavy psychological toll. The peoples of Asia and Africa shared not only in the technological revolution exported by the West, but also became infected by the Western "hang-up" on sex. An adolescent admixture of voyeurism, curiosity, exploration and exploitation had become almost universal, and Mons Pubis and Mons Veneris had become prominent cultural landmarks within the global village.

At this point, the presence of a number of priests who had made themselves "eunuchs for the sake of the Kingdom" was especially significant. These men and women were obviously psychologically whole persons, more transparently free than the great majority of those who proclaimed that freedom was to be found only in the gardens of Priapus and in the alembics of mind-exploding drugs.

Priesthood was not confined, however, to the celibate teacher-counselor who presided over the Christian assembly at the weekly liturgy. The Christian home had become the living center of the Church, in much the same way that Judaism had found the source of its continuing vitality in the home rather than in the synagogue.

For the Christian, this return to the home as an *ecclesiola,* the Church in miniature, was largely the result of sociological pressures, but the fact of the home-church had the support of the earliest Christian traditions.

Christianity had begun with the *oikos*—the Church in the home and the neighborhood, and for at least two centuries the term *church* had no association with a building specifically set aside for prayer and worship. The "sacred space" was where one lived and worked, and this ancient realization was rediscovered by Christians at the end of the twentieth century.

The Christian home became, once again, the "sacred space." Here one learned what it meant to be a Christian in the face of an indifferent, often hostile, environment outside one's home. Here one prayed in the most meaningful of communities, and celebrated daily the mystery of the Eucharist, with the father of the family, presiding as ordained priest over the liturgical assembly of his own family. In those cases where the father died before his wife, the widow was given the option of being ordained in his place, so that He might continue to be present sacramentally wherever two or three were gathered together in His name.

All of the above is, of course, but a broad projection into the future. Demography, sociology, and the documents of the Second Vatican Council give one ample warrant, however, for surmising that the future of the Christian family may follow some of the tracks of development we have tried to sketch here.

ABOUT THE AUTHORS

Clayton C. Barbeau's first nationally published article was in *America* magazine in 1955. Since then his writings have appeared in dozens of publications: *Marriage, Family Digest, The Nation, Ave Maria, National Catholic Reporter, Catholic Digest,* and *Writer's Digest.*

His novel, *The Ikon,* based on his experiences during the Korean War, was awarded the James D. Phelan prize in literature.

His book on Christian fatherhood, *The Head of The Family,* was first published in 1961, and was in its fourth printing before being brought out in a paperback Image Book in 1970. The book has since been published in the British Commonwealth, and translated into Italian.

Mr. Barbeau wrote the article, "Beat Writing," for the *New Catholic Encyclopedia,* edited the volume *Art, Obscenity and Your Children* (Abbey Press) and the recent poetry-photo book *The Generation of*

Love (Bruce Publishing). In collaboration with his wife, he recently co-authored three chapters of the interfaith book *Marriage: An Interfaith Guide for All Couples.*

He lives in Haight-Ashbury with his wife, Myra and their eight children. He recently resigned as editor of *Way/Catholic Viewpoints,* consistently a top-award winner in the Catholic Press, in order to return to full-time writing and lecturing.

Joan Bel Geddes is the author of *Small World: A History of Baby Care from the Stone Age to the Spock Age.* Daughter of Norman Bel Geddes, producer and artist, she studied sociology and economics at Columbia, has worked in theatre, industrial design, advertising, radio, television, and book and magazine publishing. The mother of three children, she has traveled extensively and written many articles on child care and family life. She is a consultant to the United Nations Children's Fund (UNICEF).

Joseph Bird, Ph.D., is a clinical psychologist and marriage counselor in Saratoga, California. He and his wife, **Lois,** are co-authors of *The Freedom of Sexual Love,* a best-selling volume on Christian marriage; *All is Love,* meditations and prayers on marriage and family life; and *Marriage is for Grown-ups.* Their writings have appeared in various periodicals. They are the parents of nine children.

William H. Bishop has contributed articles to *The Living Light, Discovery,* and *Way/Catholic Viewpoints* as well as the paperback book *Art, Obscenity and Your Children* (Abbey Press). Actively engaged in adult education work, interfaith and interracial work, Mr. Bishop is an aircraft instrument mechanic. He and his wife Adela are the parents of three children and reside in Oakland, California.

Sidney Callahan, a graduate *(magna cum laude)* from Bryn Mawr, is the authoress of *The Illusion of Eve, Beyond Birth Control,* and *The Working Mother* as well as the writer of a regular column for the *National Catholic Reporter.* She has contributed articles to various magazines on the topic of marriage and various aspects of family life. Married to Daniel Callahan, former associate editor of *Commonweal,* she is the mother of six children. Involved in local political and social issues and "the usual volunteer work," Mrs. Callahan, widely sought after as a lecturer, still lists her main occupation as mother-housewife.

"A sensitive and learned book, and—contrary to almost all books of this kind written by women—devoid of any trace of feminist resentment." So wrote the eminent psychiatrist Karl Stern about **Janet Golden's** *The Quite Possible She* (Abbey Press). This study of the difficulties and challenges confronting modern married women was Mrs. Golden's first book, but she has written book reviews and articles for various publications. She makes her home in Carmel, California, with her husband, Joseph, and three children.

Rosemary Haughton has become known to thousands of persons through one or more of her twenty-three books. In her native England, she is in demand as a participant on television talk shows, and she has lectured there and in the United States. Among her books are *The Holiness of Sex* (Abbey Press), *Act of Love, On Trying To Be Human, Why Be a Christian,* and *The Good News for Children.* The book that did more than any other, perhaps, to establish her as what theologian Charles Davis called "a writer of astonishing originality" was *The Transformation of Man.*

Married to the head of the English Department at Ampleforth College, Mrs. Haughton is the mother of ten children, ranging in age from twenty years to the youngest born in January, 1968. "I write when I can," Mrs. Haughton says, "I don't have regular times or places to write, just when I can manage it."

Eulah Laucks is a Director of the Center for the Study of Democratic Institutions (Fund for the Republic, Inc.) in Santa Barbara, California. A class of '38, *cum laude* graduate in Journalism of the University of Washington—which she was able to attend only by working as a secretary for eight years and saving her money—she spent her senior year in studies abroad. She did special studies in Journalism ("Propaganda in the Fascist Press"), Political Science ("Italian Colonial Policy in Ethiopia"), and Geography ("Economic Use of the Drained Pontine Marshes"). She returned to the U.S. just before World War II, and worked in public relations until her marriage in 1942 to Irving F. Laucks, chemist, inventor, and philanthropist. They have one daughter and raised a boy who had lost his parents. Mrs. Laucks is a regent of Immaculate Heart College in Los Angeles. Her current areas of interest are education, the role of women in contemporary life, and family life in our time.

Paul Marx, O.S.B., Ph.D., recently resigned as Chairman of the Sociology Department of St. John's University in Collegeville, Minn., in order to devote more time to research and direct work in the area of family life. **Jack Quesnell,** A.C.S.W., is Supervisor of Marriage Counseling at the Catholic Charities Bureau of Minneapolis, Minn. Mr. Quesnell is married, the father of three. The priest-sociologist, layman-marriage counselor have been a most effective team in presenting workshops on marriage and family life in our society, workshops dealing with the social and psychological as well as the moral and physical aspects of marriage. Their two workshops on marriage, and one for engaged couples, have been recorded by Argus Communications of Chicago. Their most recent collaborative effort in writing was a chapter in the book, *Moral Issues in Marriage Counseling.*

Simon Scanlon is a Franciscan friar who, prior to entering the Franciscan order, served as an artilleryman with the U.S. Army in New Guinea and the South Pacific during World War II. Ordained in 1954, he has served as a teacher, chaplain to the layman's "Third Order," and been active in Franciscan radio and television productions. A perceptive film critic, he edited the National Catholic Broadcasting Association's magazine *Gabriel* and managed the Gabriel Awards for outstanding religious television productions. Sometimes called "The Tenderloin Priest," Father Simon directs The Poverello Coffee House in San Francisco's vice-ridden Tenderloin, and The Franciscan Social Center, a meeting place for the pensioners and the lonely, in the same neighborhood. Editor of *Way/Catholic Viewpoints,* Father Simon's articles dealing with current social problems have an unusually good record of being reprinted in other publications.

Mr. and Mrs. Scharper bring to their subject a rich and varied experience in education, literature and the arts. **Philip Scharper,** previously editor-in-chief of Sheed and Ward publishers, now serves in that same capacity for Orbis Books. Formerly Assistant Professor of English at Fordham and Associate Editor of *Commonweal,* he is well known in Catholic intellectual circles through his lectures, articles, and book reviews and his frequent appearances on radio and television. Active in interfaith work, he has contributed to *The Church and the Nations, The Layman and the Church,* and was editor of *American Catholics: A Protestant-Jewish View* and *Torah and Gospel: Jewish and Catholic Theology in Dialogue.* He is the author of *Meet the American Catholic,* and has written scripts for television programs on The World Council of Churches, Communism and Christianity, and a History of Man, to name but a few. He has also appeared as an interviewer on many programs.

Sally Moorman Scharper is herself a lecturer, former professor of speech and drama and an actress. She originated on the American stage such roles as Violaine in Claudel's *The Tidings Brought to Mary*, Sister Vazous in *The Song of Bernadette*, Aunt Charity in *Sing Out Sweet Land*, and the Princess in *Lute Song*. She has appeared on numerous national radio programs; and her reading of "Peace on Earth" on The Catholic Hour drew a record mail response. She has collaborated with her husband in writing numerous television scripts on religious subjects for network production. One of these, an hour-long color presentation on the archeology of the Old Testament, was produced by NBC and has received seven national and international awards.

They are the parents of six children.